The
Mexican
Pet

Other books by Jan Harold Brunvand

THE CHOKING DOBERMAN
THE VANISHING HITCHHIKER
THE STUDY OF AMERICAN FOLKLORE
READINGS IN AMERICAN FOLKLORE

The Mexican Pet

More "New" Urban Legends and Some Old Favorites

JAN HAROLD BRUNVAND

UNIVERSITY OF UTAH

W·W·NORTON & COMPANY

New York · London

Permission to quote from the following is gratefully acknowledged:
"Laurie (Strange Things Happen)" written by Milton Addington and Cathie
Harmon. Copyright © 1965 Vogue Music & E. M. Long Music Co. (c/o The
Welk Music Group, Santa Monica, California 90401). International Copyright
secured. All rights reserved.

"Bringing Mary Home," Chaw Mack, Joe Kingston, John Duffey, © 1965 Fort
Knox Music, Inc. and Trio Music Company, Inc. All rights administered by
Hudson Bay Music, Inc. All rights reserved.

Library of Congress Cataloging in Publication Data
Brunvand, Jan Harold.
     The Mexican pet.
     Includes bibliographical references and index.
     1. Urban folklore—United States. 2. Legends—
United States. 3. Legends—United States—History
and criticism. I. Title.
GR105.B689 1986   398.2'09173'2   85-29841

ISBN 0-393-02324-9

W. W. Norton & Company, Inc., 500 Fifth Avenue, New York, N. Y. 10110
W. W. Norton & Company Ltd., 37 Great Russell Street, London WC1B 3NU

1 2 3 4 5 6 7 8 9 0

GR
105
.B689
1986

CONTENTS

♣Refers to stories in *The Vanishing Hitchhiker.*
🐕Refers to stories in *The Choking Doberman.*

5

6 CONTENTS

PREFACE

When Will It All End?

Brunvand, a professor of English and folklore at
the University of Utah, seems to have stumbled
onto a cottage industry.
—Peter Gorner in *The Chicago Tribune*
21 June 1984

How right he was! First I wrote ♣*The Vanishing Hitchhiker,* *
about the scant three dozen or so classic urban legends
that had been identified by earlier folklore scholars.
Then came a sequel, ✣*The Choking Doberman,* † with several dozen "new" urban legends, many of them sent to
me by my faithful readers; this time, I thought, I had
really done the definitive job on these true-sounding but
utterly false stories that pass from person to person even
in this modern day. But I was wrong again, as readers,
students, friends, and acquaintances were quick to in-
form me. More stories arrived, and the result is this latest
collection of about fifty even newer "new" urban leg-

---

*New York: W. W. Norton, 1981, hereinafter referred to with the
symbol ♣.
†New York: W. W. Norton, 1984, hereinafter referred to with the
symbol ✣.

ends, along with some new versions of old favorites. I'm
beginning to wonder when it will all end.

But why *should* it end? Folklore—the "oral tradition"
—never stands still for stuffing and mounting by the
experts. No sooner do we folklorists track down, record,
and publish a story, a song, or a saying than it pops up
again in a different disguise. Repetition and variation in
some traditional group and style are the very features
that define folklore, and this folk process of oral transmission and transformation defies the march of progress. In fact, folk tradition even hitchhikes along with
technological advances, so we can hear urban legends
now on radio and television, see them dramatized in
films, read them in newspapers, and transmit them to
others via the mail, computer, or telephone. What the
first stage of my cottage industry largely consists of is
merely reading my mail, following the media, and keeping my ears open for the latest "true" stories that are
going around in several different versions.

People are always telling, writing, and phoning me
these rumors and stories—wonderfully bizarre, usually
funny, sometimes horrible, often weird, but always plausible. As soon as I open a letter that begins something
like "I just read your book and I wonder if *this* one might
be an urban legend . . .," I know that I'm probably about
to read another likely candidate for my folkloristic research. As soon as someone starts telling me something
like "I don't know if this is *true,* but . . .," I've come to
expect yet another piece of data—i.e. a "new" urban
legend. I must admit that, in one form or another, I've
heard most of them before, but that's an occupational
hazard for folklorists.

"Folklore"—the material—is what goes around and
around and around by word of mouth, ever recognizable
but ever changing too. "Folklore"—the study—is what I
and my fellow researchers in this field do with it: collect

the variations, organize them, and most of all try to explain the forms this material takes and the needs it seems to fill.

This book places *texts* rather than analyses of recent urban rumors and legends in the foreground. All of these texts are "new"; that is, they are either currently circulating versions of beliefs and stories discussed in *The Vanishing Hitchhiker* and *The Choking Doberman,* or they are recent items not mentioned in my earlier books. In actuality, of course, most of the stories are "old"; that is, they represent variations on previous themes. I have added comments and notes to each text explaining this sort of thing, and the reader wanting to learn more about urban legend studies should consult my first two volumes. There, too, you will find many other familiar urban legends that I couldn't squeeze into this collection, such as ♣"The Hook," ♣"The Runaway Grandmother," ♣"Alligators in the Sewers," and ♣"The Cement-Filled Car" in *The Vanishing Hitchhiker;* and ✸"The Elephant That Sat on a VW," ✸"The Procter & Gamble Trademark," ✸"The Stuck Couple," and ✸"Superglue Revenge" in *The Choking Doberman.* The little symbols, remember, always remind you in which earlier book the stories that are presented here were discussed.

Many texts in this book, unlike in my previous two, are quoted from news media and other sources in "popular" culture rather than purely "folk" circulation. I have come to appreciate much more since I began studying urban legends how central the print and broadcast media have become in the dissemination of traditional stories. Along with the claim that these odd things supposedly happened to the proverbial friend of a friend (the foaf), the other common validating formula used when they are told is, "I think this was in the paper . . . or on the news." And since most urban legends are at least *plausible,* if a bit unlikely, most people tend to believe them at

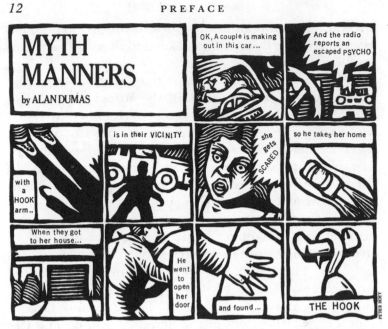

Credit: Alan Dumas and Peter Hoey

first—at least they believe *some* of the stories *some* of the time.

These stories (despite the subtitle of my first book) are not necessarily just *American* folklore. I evidently misled some readers with the line "American Urban Legends and Their Meanings." What I meant was that most of my examples were drawn from sources in the United States and analyzed in terms of modern American culture. But the urban legend *as a genre* is not an exclusive American phenomenon. Take ♣"The Death Car," for instance, which has been a favorite in the United States for at least thirty years. People tell it something like this:

There's this beautiful classic Corvette [Porsche, Thunderbird, Buick etc.] that a dealer out in _____ has been trying to get rid of for months, and he's only charging $200 [$50, $100, $500, etc.] for it! The *catch is that someone died in that car, or committed suicide or something, way out in the desert [woods, boondocks, inside his garage, etc.]. The body wasn't discovered for about a month, and the smell of death is so strong in that car that no one can stand to drive it. The stench not only permeated the upholstery but even soaked into the fiber glass body of the Corvette. So everyone that tries to drive the car brings it right back to the dealer and demands a refund. Wow, just think, a Corvette for $200! I heard this from a guy at work who knows someone who has a friend who thought he could either fumigate it or get used to the smell, but finally he had to take it back just like everyone else.*

A writer for the London *Times* (27 July 1982) reading about that one in my first book suggested that the "gorily odoriferous history" of the car tainted with the smell of death "reveals a knot of American obsessions—hygiene, money, death and automobiles." He was right about the latent themes in the story, I think, but definitely wrong about the Americanness of it, since the legend is widely told in several countries with appropriate variations in the price and model of the car and the circumstances of the death.

Another recent favorite "American" urban legend is a variation on the ♣"Hilarious Accidents" theme that centers on an exploding toilet. A typical version goes like this:

There was a guy I heard about that had to be in the hospital for something. [Often it is to recover from an earlier hilarious acident.] And while he was in there his wife decided to paint the bathroom. Well, when she finished painting, she cleaned the brushes and dumped the paint thinner in the toilet; but before she could flush it down, her husband arrived home from the hospital. The first thing he happened to want to do was to use the bathroom, so he sat down on the toilet; and he had a cigarette in his hand, so he just dropped it into the toilet at the same time. He blew himself right off the pot! So the paramedics came—or maybe it was the ambulance guys that had just brought him home—and they had to load him on the stretcher face down. Then one of the ambulance guys asked him what in the world had happened, and when he told them, they started to laugh so hard that one of them let go of the corner of the stretcher, and he fell off and broke his leg.

A legend like this makes it obvious why some journalists refer to such stories as "Mack Sennetts," in reference to the old Keystone cops movies with their slapstick scenes.* Another journalistic term for urban legends is "Red Wagon Stories," a possible reference to the red rolling ticket office in oldtime carnivals and circuses and signifying (perhaps) ballyhoo and blarney.† In Holland, incidentally, urban legends are known as *Broodje Aap,* or "Monkey Sandwiches," with reference to the story that certain sausages are made of monkey meat.‡

International though urban legends—by any name—may be, many people still seem to regard them as peculiar to the United States. To another English journalist (*Daily Telegraph,* 17 February 1983), for example, stories

---

*Columnist Al Allen of *The Sacramento Bee* used this term in his very first "On the Light Side" column in April 1970, writing about urban legends.

†Columnist Ray Orrock of The Livermore, California, *Tri-Valley Herald* brought this term to my attention but lacked for an explanation. I've also heard of a journalist calling such stories "dead catters," probably with reference to "The Dead Cat in the Package."

‡See Ethel Portnoy's book of that title, which is subtitled "De folklore van de post-industriele samenleving" (Amsterdam: Uitgeverij De Harmonie, 1978).

like "The Death Car" or "The Exploding Toilet" merely
prove how low-brow we Americans are:

> *Americans are notoriously concerned more with*
> *verisimilitude than with truth. They are*
> *gossip-mongers, collectors of scandal, thrivers on*
> *rumour, and manifest a childlike belief in any story,*
> *no matter how incredible or outrageous, so long as*
> *there are enough "facts" inserted to give it credence.*
> *. . . Americans are simply displaying a normal,*
> *unhealthy, interest in scandalous and embarrassing*
> *situations. . . . [These stories] are a sad comment on*
> *Americans' naivety and lack of self-confidence.*

The fact is that many urban legends that we tell and
believe so gullibly here in the Colonies have their counterparts, or even their prototypes, in Europe. The British
Isles are a hotbed of such stories that are purveyed not
only in oral tradition but regularly also by a daily press
always searching for fresh scandal and gags with which
to regale their eager readers. I found a lovely version of
"The Choking Doberman" right on the front page of the
stately London *Times;* and here, just for the record, is an
exploding toilet variant as told to me by an Englishman:

> *This bloke was having a crap in the local bog* and*
> *the toilet exploded underneath him. You see, the*
> *attendant had just cleaned the toilet with bleach or*
> *something, and this feller crapping caused a chemical*
> *reaction. The attendant came to the rescue, but he*
> *couldn't get into the cubicle because the door was*
> *locked, so he had to call for the fire brigade and the*

---

*Lower-class British slang for privy or toilet, the term "bog" ap-
pears in seventeenth- and eighteenth-century English sources as
"bog-house" or "bog-shop." The allusion is evidently to the soft,
dirty, "boggy" nature of an outhouse, though here the reference is
to a water closet in a public restroom.

ambulance. And when the ambulance men came they had to put this feller face down on the stretcher because his bum was too sore, and they couldn't cover it with a blanket for the same reason, and the ambulance men couldn't stop laughing, and he fell off the stretcher twice.

In case you're wondering, so far as I can tell, that story was a rural gag told about outhouses before it began to circulate as an urban legend and got adapted to American suburban bathrooms and English public "bogs." The punchline of the hoary jest, spoken by the farmer who was blown out of the privy, was this: "It must have been something I et!" With that minimal scholarly note, let us get on to some more of the stories themselves.

ACKNOWLEDGMENTS

Scores of good friends, colleagues, readers, writers, editors, students, folklorists, and other co-researchers who have sent me some of the rumors, stories, and clippings that I quote and paraphrase in this book are named where their contributions occur. I wish to thank them all once again here. Many other people have been helpful in more general and miscellaneous ways, and if I listed all of their specific contributions it would sound too much like another legend. Instead, here are simply their names, with my grateful thanks to one and all: James A. Able, Jr., Christopher Adkins, Thomas J. Allman, Dan Barnes, Mac Barrick, Neil Barron, Ervin Beck, Bob Bethke, Meg Brady, John Burrison, Charles Camp, Simon J. Carmel, Keith Cunningham, Tom Curtis, Mary Dickson, David Eisen, Karl Fleischhauer, Rochelle Goldstein, Dick Hafer, Hal Hall, James R. Halsey, Donn V. Hart, Henry Hester, Bruce Johnson, Teddi Kachi, Kevin Kelly, Steve Moorman, Don L. F. Nilsen, Ray Oliver, Storn Peterson, Lisa Ray, Jim Ruderman, Kent Shelton, John F. Sherry, Jr., Penny Street, Barre Toelken, Elaine Viets, and Tom Zaniello.

My article "Urban Legends in the Making" appeared

in No. 48 of *Whole Earth Review* (Fall 1985, pp. 124–29), and an excerpt was published earlier in the *San Francisco Chronicle* (17 July 1985). Scores of readers responded to my appeal for more information on recent urban legends, and some of the distributional patterns traced in this book are the result. As I asked there, "Write me if you've heard these." The address is:

Professor Jan Harold Brunvand
Department of English
University of Utah
Salt Lake City, UT 84112

The
Mexican
Pet

1

Animal Stories

"The Mexican Pet"

*A woman from La Mesa, California [a city east of
San Diego], went to Tijuana, Mexico, to do some
shopping. As any visitor to this border town knows,
the streets near the shopping areas are populated with
stray dogs. The woman took pity on one little stray
and offered it a few bites of her lunch, after which it
followed her around for the rest of the afternoon.*

*When it came time to return home, the woman had
become so attached to her little friend that she
couldn't bear to leave him behind. Knowing that it
was illegal to bring a dog across the international
border, she hid him among some packages on the
seat of her car and managed to pass through the
border checkpoint without incident. After arriving
home, she gave the dog a bath, brushed his fur, then
retired for the night with her newfound pet curled up
at the foot of her bed.*

*When she awoke the next morning, the woman
noticed that there was an oozing mucus around the
dog's eyes, and a slight foaming at the mouth. Afraid
that the dog might be sick, she rushed him to a*

*nearby veterinarian and returned home to await word
on her pet's condition.*

*The call soon came. "I have just one question,"
said the vet. "Where did you get this dog?"*

*The woman didn't want to get into trouble, so she
told the vet that she had found the dog running loose
in the street near her home in La Mesa.*

*But the vet didn't buy it. "You did not find this dog
in La Mesa. Where did you get this dog?"*

*The woman nervously admitted having brought the
dog across the border from Tijuana. "But tell me,
doctor," she said. "What's wrong with my dog?"*

*His reply was brief and to the point: "First of all,
it's not a dog—it's a Mexican sewer rat. And second,
it's dying."*

(This version was sent to me by Mike Milch of Newport
Beach, California, who heard it from his sister in San
Diego, as she had been told it as a true story by a co-
worker around February, 1984.)

I first began to notice "The Mexican Pet" in Autumn
1983, both in Utah and in letters from several states. The
pet may be picked up in Acapulco (from the ocean), in
Mexico City (near an open-air restaurant), or from the
unpaved street of a village. Usually the tourist tries in
broken Spanish to find out who owns the animal before
carrying it off. Then it is kept in the hotel room for the
rest of the vacation. Often the rat is specifically said to
be mistaken for a Chihuahua or Mexican Hairless, and
generally the woman smuggles it home held close to her
body—under her coat or sweater, in her purse, or the
like. Back home, in some versions, the pet is found
drowned in the toilet bowl, and then its body is taken to
the vet for an explanation; in other tellings the Mexican
pet fights with two resident pets, and then all three are

taken in for treatment. The vet says, "This one is a cat, this one is a dog, but *this* one is a sewer rat! What in the world are you doing with it?" Usually the tourist simply brings the new pet in for its shots, and in a couple of versions the vet then grabs the animal and snaps its neck before explaining the problem. The pet is sometimes described as "a Mexican long-haired rat." A few informants claim that their sources can furnish a photograph of the tourist posing with "little Chico," but I have yet to see one. A version incorporated into "The Real Talking People Show" presented in Vancouver, B.C., by Tamahnous Theatre in 1984 has the pet smuggled across two international borders into Canada.

Besides the wide distribution of the same story in slightly different unverifiable versions, "The Mexican Pet" has other obvious hallmarks of the modern urban legend. It deals with a mishap during a vacation to Mexico, just like ♣"The Runaway Grandmother"; it mentions a sewer, as in ♣"Alligators in the . . . "; and it describes getting up close to a rat, as in ♣"The Kentucky Fried Rat." Grotesque problems with pets are found in several other legends in this chapter, and the speaking role for a veterinarian is a recent feature reminiscent of "The Choking Doberman" legend.

"The Kangaroo Thief"

A group of tourists driving through the Australian outback run down a kangaroo. For a joke, one props the roo against a post and drapes his coat over its shoulders to pose for a photograph. Suddenly the kangaroo wakes up and bounds away, carrying the man's wallet and passport into oblivion.

(As published in the Sydney *Sunday Herald* for 22 May 1983, based on versions sent in by three different readers.)

Some Americans claim it was the Kingston Trio touring in Australia who had this experience. The story has its western American counterpart in one I call "The Bear Kidnapper":

A family driving through Yellowstone Park stops to photograph a bear. The animal seems so placid and harmless that mother puts the baby either on the bear's back or in its arms for a cute posed picture. While they are focusing the camera, the bear turns and walks into the forest taking baby along.

There's yet another variant of this legend, which we might call "The Deer Departed":

A proud hunter has downed a huge deer [or moose] with an impressive rack of antlers. He straightens out the animal's head and places his expensive high-powered rifle with its powerful telescopic sight across the antlers for the traditional photograph. Just as he has arranged his camera on the tripod, set the automatic timer, and started forward to pose with his kill, the animal revives, having only been stunned; it leaps to its feet and dashes off into the woods with the rifle still firmly in place.

For another story of poetic justice involving an animal versus man, see "The Animal's Revenge" below. The Yellowstone Park story is mentioned in *The Choking Doberman,* chapter 2. Considering all the urban legends in which pets suffer, it's nice to see some winners among the beasts now and then.

"The Giant Catfish"

*There was some kind of problem with the dam at a
reservoir in the Midwest or South, and a couple of
divers were hired to go down and check into it. They
had only been underwater a short time before they
came rushing back up to the surface, and they were
really upset about something—absolutely pale as
death and shaking all over. It seems that they had
seen some giant catfish [or carp] down there in the
deepest part of the lake, right up next to the dam.
These catfish were so huge that they could easily
swallow a man! The divers refused to go back down,
or even to dive again anywhere, and both of them had
their hair turn white overnight from the scare they
had suffered in those murky waters.*

Generally some local and fairly small lake is identified
as the actual site of this adventure, although only the
usual friend of a friend is given as the source of the story.
I have heard "The Giant Catfish" described as "an article of faith in many parts of Arkansas, Tennessee, Kentucky, and Southern Illinois," but, indeed, it is known
almost everywhere in the United States, always localized
to some specific place like Tuttle Creek Reservoir, Kansas; Elephant Butte Reservoir, New Mexico; Roosevelt
Lake, Arizona; and, of course, the Mississippi River
throughout its length. Even if people are not convinced
by the diver story, they do believe in catfish as big as dogs
(people, calves, Volkswagens, etc.) that can devour a
swimmer (chew off a leg, etc.). Sometimes the horrible
fright or injury is said to have taken place near a lock
rather than a dam, and I have heard versions associated

with marine monsters near Texas gulf coast oil platforms and the sunken USS *Arizona* at Pearl Harbor.

Jon M. Graznak of Columbia, Missouri, a fisheries biologist, had heard giant catfish stories since his childhood in Alabama. In about the mid-1970s he began to keep closer records of them. He reported to me in November 1985, after talking to thirty-eight powerhouse superintendents (most of whom had heard the stories), that "None claimed to have firsthand knowledge, and only two had ever been in a powerhouse where any type of underwater maintenance was even required." Graznak also wrote, "I have met only one person who claims to have been one of the divers. However, the individual was remarkably drunk at the time, and I believe that if I had continued the conversation, he might well have claimed to be the fish."

Perhaps this legend is the rural counterpart of the legend that giant alligators infest the sewers of New York City. The certain clue that we are dealing with folklore here, besides the many variations, is the mention of the old hair-turned-white motif, which regularly occurs—not in real life, but only in legends—especially the stories describing grisly crimes or gruesome accidents.

"The Can of Snakes"

A couple of men walking along a stream bank to do some fishing see a little boy sitting there with his fishline in the water and a can of bait on the ground next to him. One of them asks the lad how the fish are biting, and he replies "Well, the fish aren't biting so well, but the worms sure are." The men chuckle about this odd answer as they continue along their way, but coming back later in the day they notice the boy slumped down in the same place he had been sitting before. He is unconscious, and they see that his hands and forearms are full of bite marks. Checking the bait can, they discover that he has been using baby copperheads [rattlesnakes, water moccasins, cottonmouths, etc.] for bait, thinking them to be worms. They rush him to a hospital in their car but arrive there too late to save his life.

Folklorist Oliver Finley Graves reports on a dozen versions of this legend, which I too have heard several times, in an article titled "The Bed of Snakes Motif in Southern Folklore" that appeared in *Southern Folklore Quarterly*, vol. 42 (1978), pp. 337–359. Among other treatments of the same motif are the following two quoted by Graves.

"The Hapless Waterskier"

I heard this story when I was in about the sixth grade or in about 1966. It occurred at Guntersville Lake [Alabama] over on the back waters where there's still tree trunks and things like that. Under the surface of the water it's pretty shallow, and it seems that there's a barbed wire fence that is still stretched under there from when before the waters were backed up that far. One time these people were skiing back over there, and this guy was skiing, and they made a wide turn into this area and he got caught on the barbed wire—this old rusty barbed wire that was still submerged under the water. And when he fell, he fell into a bed of snakes—water moccasins or something like that. When they came back around to get him he started hollering, and when they got to him they found that he'd been bitten about forty or fifty times and he died from this accident.

"The Incautious Swimmer"

*Some boys went swimming in Piney Creek. They
got out of the car and one yelled, "Last one in is a
rotten egg!" He jumped in first, but he yelled "Go
back, go back!" Later, when they got him out, they
found that he had been bitten by many snakes. My
father used to tell this to me as a warning about just
jumping in to swim.*

Graves points out that Willie Morris mentioned "The
Hapless Waterskier" in his *North toward Home* (1967),
while Lisa Alther described "The Incautious Swimmer"
in her novel *Kinflicks* (1976).

The more urban treatment of the bed of snakes motif
is the legend about a person bitten by water snakes that
infest an amusement park ride. Usually it is a fun house
or tunnel-of-love ride that transports people in little
boats through darkened passageways. Someone dangles
a hand over the side, and snakes that have moved into
the warm waters inside for the winter begin to bite. The
rider may emerge at the other end of the ride already
dead. Possibly the *suburban* version of the story is ♣"The
Snake in the Blanket," which is about a woman bitten by
a baby poisonous snake that was sewn into an imported
blanket, coat, or sweater during its manufacture in the
Far East. The item is displayed for sale in a discount
store at a local shopping mall. While running her hand
over the material, the shopper feels a tiny pinprick that
later proves to be a snakebite. She is usually saved from
death by a timely diagnosis and the rushing in of the
required antidote. Another snake legend is given in
chapter 5.

♣ "The Dead Cat in the Package"

BLOOMINGTON, IND. *The couple, after shopping on Bloomington's eastside, stopped for a bite at a fast food restaurant. As they left their car in the parking lot they saw a dead cat on the pavement.*

"Please," the woman said, "we just can't leave the poor thing there to be squashed. Can't we do something?"

The man rearranged the groceries in the car and produced a large sack into which he placed the body of the cat. He put the sack on the hood of his car, and the couple went into the restaurant.

From their seats they could see another woman approaching through the parking lot. As she passed the car she paused, looked around, and picked up the sack.

She too entered the restaurant and placed the sack on the floor beside her booth. As she made her way through her meal, curiosity overcame her.

She leaned over, peered into the sack, and fainted dead away.

The manager called the ambulance which arrived within minutes from its station a couple of blocks away.

Attendants gathered up the woman and her personal effects.

As they placed her unconscious body into the ambulance, the sack containing the dead cat was perched in the middle of her chest.

(Quoted from Bill Pittman's column in the *Indianapolis News,* 29 January 1983.)

This is where I came in! I collected my first version of this venerable urban legend from the Bloomington, Indiana, *Daily Herald-Telephone* in May 1959 when it was alleged to have happened in Indianapolis. There are literally hundreds of texts and scores of variations of it that are repeated all over the country.

As told in the 1950s, the story usually described a woman living in a city apartment whose cat died. Lacking a suitable place to bury her pet, she called a friend in the suburbs who agreed to meet her in a downtown department store, receive a package containing the furry little corpse, and bury it at home in her garden. The package is stolen, and the pet owner later sees the thief—a sweet little old lady—being revived after fainting.* More recent twists in the plot, as shown above, are finding the cat already dead (or driving over it on the way to go shopping), putting it into a sack (often one bearing the name of a fashionable shop), and observing the thief looking into the sack and fainting. A typical example of this later version, as it was published in a Massachusetts newspaper in December 1982, is reprinted in *The Choking Doberman*. Another appeared on 4 February 1985 in John Ladue's column "In My Opinion" published in the Plattsburgh, New York, *Press-Republican*. The old legend is not extinct; but there's more.

A New York City variation describes a woman struggling in the subway with a large suitcase that gets stolen from her by a young man who pretends to be helping her get it through the turnstile. Once she gets to the other side, he turns and runs away with the suitcase. It contains

---

*Professor Thomas Fox Averill of Washburn University, Topeka, Kansas, used a version of this kind that he heard in 1975 as the basis for a short story titled "Helen Singleton and the Dead Cat." This first appeared in *Cimarron Review* (No. 46, January 1979) and then in Fox's collection *Passes at the Moon* (Topeka: Woodley Press, 1985), pp. 17–27.

Credit: *Bum (Brighten Up Monday) Stories* by Dick Bothwell (Great Outdoors Publishing Co., 1978)

the body of her late Great Dane, which she was taking to the pet cemetery.

An even older form of "The Dead Cat in the Package," which I have traced back to around 1906, describes the bereaved pet owner trying in various ways to dispose of the cat package but always being foiled somehow by a helpful stranger. At the end of the day he or she still has the package, which is then opened for one more tearful look at poor pussy. But instead of a cat corpse, the package is now found to contain a large ham or a nice leg of mutton. Humorist Alexander King told a story on himself in *May This House Be Safe from Tigers* (New York:

Simon and Schuster, 1960) in which his package containing two dead kittens for disposal accidentally got switched with a package containing steaks. King implied that this "fantastic and improbable thing . . . actually occurred" to him in the early 1920s.

A song in Cockney dialect titled "The Body in the Bag" tells nearly the same story as the dead cat legend. The words and music are given "with some additions by Eric Winter from childhood recollection" in the English journal *Sing* (vol. 5, July 1960, p. 47), based on an earlier printing in *Singabout*. In this variation a man carries the supposedly dead body of his pet around all day in a bag, trying to dispose of it. At the end of the day, having failed to do so, he hears a plaintive meow from the bag and opens it to find seven newborn kittens there.

The latest revision of the plot concerns some baggage handlers for an international airline flying out of Chicago who find a dead poodle in a crate they are loading on a flight to Rome. Fearing they might be sued for letting the dog die, they secure a similar one from a kennel and substitute it. When the owner comes to recover her crate at the terminal in Rome, she faints in terror when the dog bounds out of its crate and licks her face, because she was shipping her *dead* pet back home to Italy for burial.

Exploding Animals

EXHIBIT A: *An elderly woman brings her beloved pet canary in to the student-run free clinic of a veterinary college for treatment of its seriously broken wing. The students decide they should cauterize the region as part of their treatment. First they anesthesize the bird with ether, then they reach for an electric cautery, forgetting that a bird's bones are hollow. The highly flammable ether has entered the broken bones, and when the tool is applied the bird immediately bursts into a ball of flame, leaving nothing behind but a small pile of scorched feathers.*

EXHIBIT B: *Another elderly woman had baked some fruit pies and set them out on a windowsill to cool while vacuuming her rugs. A swarm of bees zoomed in and settled on the pies, so she used her vacuum cleaner to swoop them up. Then, realizing that she had a bag full of angry bees to get rid of, she turned on the gas in her oven without lighting it and held the vacuum cleaner hose over the jet, thus thinking to kill the bees. Shortly afterward she turned the cleaner back on to continue her work, and it exploded.*

The classic story in this category is ▲"The Microwaved Pet or Baby." Human counterparts to the pet tragedies are an exploding patient story that I call ➤"The Proctological Examination" and ➤"The Death of Little Mikey," about which the less said the better. (A brief note on an actual ruptured stomach incident involving sodium bicarbonate and water is given in *Science News,* vol. 126, [1984] p. 360.) If you get a bang out of this sort of yarn, see *The Choking Doberman* for further details.

⋙"The Animal's Revenge"

RABBIT REVENGE

*This one's got the feel of an urban folktale to us—
no names, no date, vague source—but we'll report it
anyway because if it's not true it ought to be.
According to a short item in* New Scientist *(vol. 103,
no. 1417, August 1984), which they attribute to "a
free magazine distributed to Australian expatriates in
London," two men in South Australia recently paid
handsomely for a little mindless cruelty they cooked
up for a rabbit they caught. The men decided to strap
a stick of the high explosive gelignite to the rabbit,
light the fuse, and set the animal free. However, they
didn't count on the frightened animal taking cover
under their four-wheel-drive vehicle. The men
escaped injury, but their $20,000 vehicle didn't. It was
demolished.*

(From *East West Journal,* March 1985, p. 13.)

Both *National Lampoon* (August 1985) and *Penthouse*
(November 1985) carried illustrated reports of this story.

In *The Choking Doberman,* chapter 2, I call this story
"The Coyote's Revenge," giving a version from
Colorado in which a man ties dynamite to the animal
only to have it run under his new camper and destroy it.
I also cite a 1973 printed version from North Carolina in
which a captured chickenhawk tied to a stick of dynamite
flies atop a farmhouse and blows the roof off. But there's
more to this; hence my more general title now. First,
another rabbit version:

*Two bachelor farmers in their early sixties were
living and farming in the extreme southeastern tip of
Nebraska near the Iowa–Missouri–Nebraska junctures.
Supposedly one of them had gone into Missouri
where large fireworks are legal and had purchased a
number of M-1000s—almost as powerful as a stick of
dynamite.*

*One of the farmers had just purchased a new
Toyota pickup truck with fiber glass shell over the
bed, and these two had driven into the countryside
for a little Fourth of July mischief. The setting was
reportedly the Barada Hills, adjacent to the Missouri
River just North of Falls City, Nebraska.*

*These two bachelors had trapped several rabbits
from woodpiles in the hills, and while drinking heavily
would tape these M-1000s to a rabbit, light the fuse,
turn the rabbit loose, and watch the rabbit blow up as
it scampered away. But one of the rabbits, instead of
running away from these two, ran instead under the
brand-new pickup truck. The explosion destroyed the
truck completely and started a grass and brush fire.
The two bachelors then found a tractor hooked to a
disc and borrowed it to disc a wide firebreak around
the fire to contain it. The way I heard it, the story was
so detailed it even had the men drinking peppermint
schnapps.*

(In a letter from Paul M. Conley of Lincoln, Nebraska,
who commented, "I was so convinced the story I had
heard was real I telephoned the Richardson County sheriff's office to verify the story. . . . But the sheriff had
heard another version in a different part of Nebraska. I'm
afraid it's just an urban legend beyond verification.")

Really, this turns out to be more of a *rural* legend
brought up to date than a truly urban legend. Vance

Randolph in his book *The Talking Turtle and other Ozark Folk Tales* (New York: Columbia University Press, 1957, pp. 123–124) gives a version under the title "Cruelty to Animals" collected in Missouri in 1932. Here a ball of rags soaked in oil is tied to a dog and set afire. The dog crawls under a house where the rags burn loose; then it runs out the other side, leaving the house in flames. Randolph mentions a variant in which boys set fire to a rabbit, which burns a hay barn down, and he cites a printed chickenhawk version from 1950.

In his notes to the Ozark tale, Herbert Halpert identifies the Old World story from which these American versions all undoubtedly derive: it is under motif J2101.1, "Lighting the cat's tail," a story traceable in Europe and beyond. In an 1888 version from Kashmir a flaming cat sets a thatched roof afire and eventually burns down a whole village. Listed under a different motif (K2351.1.) is the version of the legend known in England as "The Sparrows of Cirencester"; in the *Motif-Index* summary, "Fire is attached to birds who fly in and set fire to a besieged city." This strategy was attributed in the Middle Ages not only to Vikings attacking English villages but, according to an Icelandic history of the early thirteenth century, to the Norwegian King Harald Hardrada laying siege to a town in Sicily. The possibility of an even older prototype is suggested by the passage in Judges (chapter 15, verses 4–5) where Samson captured three hundred foxes (how?), tied firebrands to their tails, and "let them go into the standing corn of the Philistines," burning their crops to the ground.

Recent American versions tend to be told as hunting or camping adventures, such as those quoted above, in which wild animals (sometimes raccoons, chipmunks, squirrels, or porcupines) are caught and tortured, with the ultimate punishment falling on the tormenters themselves. Naturally, the vehicle or cabin destroyed is always

HUNTERS' CRUEL TRICK BACKFIRES

A SADISTIC STUNT WITH GELIGNITE AND A CAPTIVE RABBIT BLEW UP IN THE FACES OF TWO PRANKSTER RABBITERS.

TWO MEN ON A SPOTLIGHTING EXPEDITION REPORTEDLY TIED A STICK OF GELIGNITE TO A RABBIT THEY HAD CAUGHT BY HAND. THE FUSE WAS LIT AND THE RABBIT RE-LEASED.

LAUGHTER EVAPORATED AS IT DOUBLED BACK AND HOPPED FOR COVER UNDER THEIR TOYOTA FOUR-WHEEL-DRIVE UTILITY.

As seen in *National Lampoon*

brand-new and expensive. There is also a fish version of the story in which an explosive is either tied to or fed to a fish, which then swims under the boat. Here's a recent published example of that variation:

Retribution for human attack upon sharks takes a variety of forms aside from the animal simply turning on its tormentor. On 25 July 1970 off Quinby, Virginia, a "playful" sport fisherman stuffed a troop-training firecracker (large cherry bomb) into the mouth of a small shark and threw it back into the water to see what would happen. And he didn't have to wait long! The shark swam under the vessel, the firecracker went off, and the 43-foot diesel powerboat promptly sank with a hole blown in a couple of bottom planks. The skipper figured $2,000 worth of repairs to his engine alone, plus replacement of broken planks and whatever had to be done to tanks, batteries, wiring, bilge pumps, and cabins. All because some "playful sport" wanted to see what it would be like to blow up a little 5-pound shark.

(From H. David Baldridge, *Shark Attack* [New York: Berkley Medallion Books, 1974], p. 117.)

Jack London's short story "Moon-Face," published in 1902, may be based on this legend. The narrator contrives to murder a man who catches trout by tossing dynamite into a deep pool. His scheme is to give the poacher a dog that has been highly trained to retrieve; then, when the dynamite stick is tossed out, the dog brings it directly back to its new master. The verdict of a coroner's jury is "death from accident while engaged in illegal fishing."

✈"The Choking Doberman"

*A woman came home from a shopping trip, loaded
with parcels, and she found her Doberman pinscher
lying in the hall gagging and choking. She dropped
her packages and tried to clear the dog's throat, but
without success; so she picked up her pet, rushed
back to her car, and sped to the veterinarian.*

*The vet took one look at the wheezing watchdog
and said that he'd probably have to operate in order
to remove whatever was blocking the dog's windpipe.
He said that the owner should go home and wait for
his call. The Doberman continued to choke and gag
in a most pitiful manner, growing weaker by the
minute.*

*The woman drove directly back home, and as soon
as she got out of her car she heard her telephone
ringing ["ringing off the hook!" people say when they
tell this story]. She opened her front door and
grabbed the phone; it was the vet, highly excited.
"Listen carefully," he said in a tone of great urgency.
"I want you to hang up the phone when I tell you to;
then don't say a word, but turn around and run
straight out of the door again. Go to a neighbor's and
wait for the police to arrive; I've called them. Now!
Don't say a word and don't hesitate, just get right out
of there!"*

*The woman was greatly alarmed at the vet's
message and his manner, but she was also very
impressed. So she wasted no time in following the
orders, and in a few minutes a police car came
screaming up. The police explained that the vet had
found two fingers stuck in her dog's throat ["two*

human *fingers," storytellers often say], and he figured that someone must have been trying to break into her home when the Doberman caught him. He might still be there. The police searched the place and found a man in her bedroom closet, cowering back in a corner in a state of shock. He was trying desperately to stop the flow of blood from his right hand, from which two fingers had been neatly nipped off.*

This one has been rampant for the past few years—the story, I mean, not the dog, for it's a completely fictional adventure that is often attributed to a friend of a friend of the narrator's source who actually was supposed to have had the experience herself.

The underlying story of an intruder found hiding in the intended victim's car or home is familiar in two other urban legends: ♣"The Killer in the Backseat" and ♣"The Babysitter and the Man Upstairs." In the first of these the warning to the woman of a man lurking in her car comes either from another motorist or from a gas station attendant; in the second story there is a telephoned warning from the police or from a telephone operator saying that threatening calls have been coming from the upstairs extension phone. But "The Choking Doberman," despite these overlaps, has its own separate history and development, as I show in detail in my book of the same title. Part of the convincing nature of the story is that Doberman pinchers are generally believed to be vicious and unpredictable dogs, though it's not clear how—or *why*—a dog would bite off one or more fingers instead of snapping at the intruder's clothing or his leg. A common Doberman scare story is that someone's pet jumped into the crib and chewed up the new baby when the nursery door was left open.

Variations on the basic themes in the legend are common. Different numbers of fingers—or even a whole hand—are said to have been bitten off. The intruder's hiding places range from closets and basements to under a bed or in a poolside cabana. There may be a trail of blood leading to his place of concealment. Sometimes the intruder has fled, but the police find him later by checking hospital emergency rooms in the area or even by taking prints from the severed fingers and sending them to the FBI. Often the tellers of this legend, who are usually white persons themselves, will specify that the fingers were those of a black, or less commonly those of a Chicano person. Occasionally "The Choking Doberman" is localized with references to names of specific victims or a local veterinarian, but no firsthand participant in the events described has ever been found. A good example of tailoring the legend to fit events is the following version and a description of its telling sent to me in June 1983 by Andrew Jones, an economist at the Centre for Urban and Regional Development Studies at Newcastle University in England:

The following story was told to a group of friends and myself on June 1st during the run-up to our recent general election. The storyteller, who works as a social worker, had spent many evenings campaigning for the Labour Party. He claimed to have heard of an incident which had happened during the previous week in North Shields and told it as a cautionary tale to others of us involved in canvassing. The gist of the tale was as follows:

A North Shields woman had returned home from work to find her pet dog lying seriously ill in her hallway. She rushed the dog to a local vet who performed an immediate tracheotomy. The horrific outcome of the operation was the discovery of a pair of human fingers lodged in the unfortunate dog's throat. The human victim of the incident was assumed to be an electioneer pushing leaflets through letterboxes. Not surprisingly, no such mutilated campaigner had been known to have turned up at any local hospitals.

The fingers-through-the-mailslot variation of the guard dog attack story is known in the United States as well, and this whole tradition, of course (and as usual), consists of old folk stories with some new twists. As I show in my second urban legend book, there are two major strands involved, one of them based on the hand-injury theme and the other the theme of a helpful animal that is misunderstood.

At the root of the injured-hand stories may lie the ancient legend about a witch who takes on an animal form and who receives a stab wound to her "paw" that can later be recognized in a corresponding wound to the witch's own hand. The supernatural motif of shape-shifting drops out in various accounts of would-be robbers injured in their hands or fingers when they stick them into a door or window with the intent of gaining unlawful entry in order to commit a robbery. Other severed-finger variants involve hands of criminals thrust out toward moving vehicles, a theme that manifests itself clearly in the urban legend "The Hook." (See also chapter 2.)

The helpful animals in age-old folk fables are of various species (dogs, hunting hawks, even snakes), but they have in common being misunderstood by the human beings whom they are attempting to guard. A classic European manifestation of this legend is the Welsh "Llewellyn and Gellert," in which the faithful hunting hound Gellert is found bloodied and gasping in the hall of Prince Llewellyn's home. The dog is presumed to have killed the baby it was left to guard, whose overturned crib is seen through the open doorway. The dog is slain, but the baby is found unharmed; and the hidden intruder

that Gellert had defended the infant from—a huge wolf
—is found inside the house dead from the dog's defen-
sive efforts.* This story is told on both sides of the Atlantic, having migrated from Wales to the United States and
Canada, where it underwent changes leading to versions
like "The Trapper and His Dog," in which the princely
trappings are replaced with appropriate frontier motifs.

As the two strands of the tradition combined to form
a story of fingers severed by a misunderstood guarding
dog from an intruder who is discovered later, various
up-to-date details such as veterinarians, the police, and
telephones creep into the folklore. And in yet another
permutation of many of these themes, a legend I call ⭢
"The Elevator Incident" injects the racism of the "black-
fingers" versions into a comical story about a black man
and his dog, in which the command "Sit!" (to the dog)
is misunderstood by three white women on the same
elevator who themselves sit down on the floor. (As mentioned in chapter 7, this incident is often, and incorrectly, credited to Reggie Jackson. More recently it has
been told on Lionel Richie.)

The whole complicated (and partly hypothetical) history of this narrative tradition may be suggested by the
diagram on page 46.

The dissemination of "The Choking Doberman" legend has been buttressed over the years by numerous
printed accounts, usually newspaper stories debunking a

---

*Although revered by many in Wales as an ancient national legend
—or even as history—the story of Llewellyn and Gellert is, as Welsh
historian Prys Morgan phrased it, "of course all moonshine, or more
exactly, a clever adaptation of a well-known international folktale."
See his essay on "The Hunt for the Welsh Past in the Romantic
Period" in Eric Hobsbawn and Terence Ranger, *The Invention of Tradition* (Cambridge: Cambridge University Press, 1983), p. 87. See *The
Choking Doberman,* chapter 1, for details of the wider tradition of this
story.

HAND INJURY THEME **MISUNDERSTOOD ANIMAL THEME**

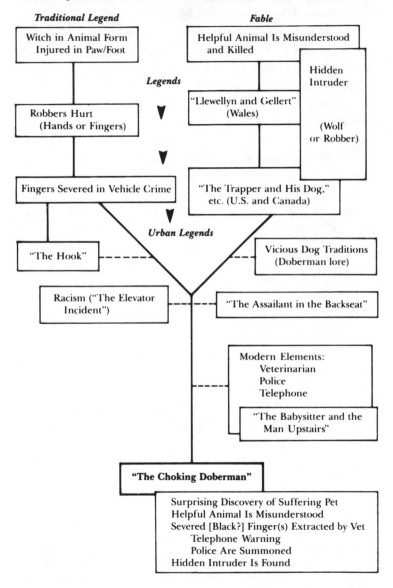

local appearance of the unverifiable tale. Recently there have been other publications (besides my own) of the same story. The Dutch artist Rien Poortvliet (illustrator of *Gnomes*) included a version about a dog of the Bouvier breed in his 1983 book *Dogs*. Second, Hilma Wolitzer had a character tell a choking-Doberman variation in her 1983 novel *In the Palomar Arms* (New York: Farrar, Straus & Giroux). A third published version of the legend appears in Rick Boyer's mystery novel *The Penny Ferry* (New York: Houghton Mifflin, 1984). Though oral tradition hardly seems to need the help of print to keep this story alive, help is being provided nonetheless.

2

Automobiles

♣"The Vanishing Hitchhiker" (A Romanian Version)

Late one spring night a mechanic driving into the capital from the city of Ploeşti to the north saw two young and beautiful women standing at the side of the road looking sadly at a flat tire on their car. He stopped and offered them a ride into town, and they gratefully directed him to the ten-story apartment building in Bucharest where they lived.

Invited in to have a cup of coffee, the man was brought to an apartment on the seventh floor. First he went into the bathroom to wash his hands, and there he removed his watch—an Omega— absentmindedly leaving it on the glass shelf above the wash basin.

Time passed quickly in pleasant conversation with the two women, and the man found himself staying all night. So, at seven in the morning he went directly to work from the apartment, realizing shortly after he arrived that he had left his watch behind.

After work that day he returned to the apartment, but the doorman for the building said that the two women he sought no longer lived there, having been killed in an automobile accident three weeks earlier on the highway near Ploeşti. They were buried, he said, in the Tincăbeşti cemetery (close to where he had offered them a ride) on the northern outskirts of Bucharest. The man protested that he had been with the women the night before in their apartment, but the doorman said this was impossible and showed him the seals that had been placed on their front door by a lawyer, pending the settlement of their estate.

Later, with the attorney's help, the man was allowed to break the seals and open the apartment door. He found his watch just where he had left it in the bathroom.

(Paraphrased from a scene in the mystery novel *Reversul medaliei* ["The Reverse Side of the Medal"] by Nicolae Mărgeanu, published in Bucharest in 1979.)

This literary episode, which a folklorist easily recognizes as a variation of the classic "Vanishing Hitchhiker" legend, was the subject of a minor controversy in 1980 when the Romanian cultural journal *Contemporanul* published a note calling attention to a closely similar scene in another recent popular novel and suggesting the possibility of plagiarism. As Liviu Poenaru pointed out in a letter to *Contemporanul* published in the 23 July 1980 issue (p. 2), the 1973 novel by D. R. Popescu titled *Vinatoarea regala* ("The Royal Hunt") contained very much the same episode. The major differences in detail were only that the driver himself had the car breakdown and he was given a ride in a car with two women in the backseat who proved to be ghosts; then he left behind on their coffee table, and later recovered, his silver cigarette case.

The explanation of this suspicious case of "accidental resemblances" of plots, as Poenaru termed it, was most likely folklore, not literary thievery, since not only are other variations on this story of the disappearing hitchhikers current in modern Romanian oral tradition, but the same basic plot circulates in international folklore. The two key elements of the widespread folk tradition present here are that the hitchhikers give an address by means of which the driver learns that they were ghosts, and a token is left behind that seems to further validate the truth of the strange experience. In most American versions it is the hitchhiker herself who leaves a borrowed coat or sweater behind, draped over her tombstone in the cemetery.

Three other features characteristic of the wider tradition are: (1) certain prophetic statements sometimes made by the hitchhiker ("Jesus is coming soon!" "The war will end by late summer," "Mount St. Helens will erupt again," etc.); (2) further identification by means of a photograph or portrait of the deceased; and (3) an association of the ghost with a particular local automobile accident that supposedly occurred on the very date of the pick-up several years earlier.

Whether the phantom rider is said to be "Resurrection Mary" in southwest Chicago, "Hitchhike Annie" in northside St. Louis, "Jesus on the Thruway" in upstate New York, "the lady of White Rock Lake" near Dallas, a ghost nun in several states, or another imagined personage in scores of other places, "The Vanishing Hitchhiker" persists as one of America's most durable modern legends. And whether exported from the United States or native to other countries (and folklorists are far from sure about this), the same sort of phantom continues to be well known abroad as well. (There was a "hitchhiking Archangel Gabriel" report widely circulated in the news media from Bavaria in late 1982, for example.) In the south Pacific—in both Hawaii and Guam—the American vanishing hitchhiker has merged with old native mythology to form a vanishing-hitchhiking-local-spirit tradition of recent legends.

"The Vanishing Hitchhiker" has entered popular culture from the folk tradition in the United States and elsewhere, just as in Romania. Several short stories, television plots, and popular songs are based on the theme, including this haunting (or haunted?) ballad recorded by pop singer Dickey Lee in 1965:

Laurie
(Strange Things Happen)

Last night at the dance I met Laurie
So lovely and warm, an angel of a girl.
Last night I fell in love with Laurie;
Strange things happen in this world.

As I walked her home she said it was her birthday.
I pulled her close and said, "Will I see you any
    more?"
Then, suddenly she asked for my sweater
And said that she was very very cold.

I kissed her goodnight at her door and started home,
Then thought about my sweater and went right back
    instead.
I knocked at her door and a man appeared.
I told why I'd come, then he said:

"You're wrong, son, you weren't with my daughter.
How can you be so cruel to come to me this way?
My Laurie left this world on her birthday.
She died a year ago today."

A strange force drew me to the graveyard.
I stood in the dark, I saw the shadows wave. . . .
And then I looked and saw my sweater,
    lying there upon her grave!
Strange things happen in this . . . [pause] worrrrrld!

(Written by Addington and Harman, published by
E. M. Long and Golddust, and recorded by Dickey Lee
as a 45 single numbered TCF [Twentieth Century Fox]
102.)

Another pop song version of the legend recorded about
the same time by the group The Country Gentlemen has
this concluding verse:

> Well, thirteen years ago today,
> In a wreck just down the road,
> Our darling Mary lost her life,
> And we miss her so.
> But thank you for your troubles,
> And the kindness you have shown,
> You're the thirteenth one who's been here,
> Bringing Mary home.

Yet another variation on the theme is singer Red Sou-
vine's trucker-song "Big Joe and Phantom 409" in which
the ghost of Big Joe, who died while swerving his huge
rig so as to miss hitting a school bus, gives rides to
occasional hitchhikers and drops them off with a dime for
a cup of coffee at a truck stop near the accident site. The
rider then learns the identity of his benefactor from the
truck-stop manager. The same story provided the Large
Marge sequence in the 1985 film *Pee-Wee's Big Adventure*.

Hundreds of vanishing-hitchhiker texts have been collected (see both of my earlier books). Most of them are
simply recombinations of familiar folk motifs told and
retold as the unverified experiences of friends of friends
—or simply as good ghost stories. But a few versions
differ from the folk tradition in significant details and are
told as actual first- or secondhand happenings. In these
puzzling cases there are no references to prophecies,
portraits, tokens, or other motifs of the folk versions, but
usually just a straightforward account of picking up a

hitchhiker who then mysteriously vanishes. Researchers in the paranormal naturally have been attracted to this theme, with the most complete review of the material being Michael Goss's 1984 book *The Evidence for Phantom Hitch-Hikers.* * Goss expressed the general frustration of the scientific approach to ghosthunting in these words:

> *The parapsychologist who dares to tackle such a case will not find this state of affairs to his liking. For every fact that he manages to align with another, there will be a contradiction somewhere else; for every fact he manages to plug into gaps left by the printed accounts, there will be one that refuses to become involved. Small wonder incidents of this kind are usually left to folklorists (p. 74).*

After a diligent search for informants with personal vanishing-hitchhiker experiences, Goss was able to isolate only five cases that seemed to "carry some degree of conviction." During his research he eliminated from consideration the instances where folk tradition had obviously corrupted people's reports of events or where there might have been deliberate lying or even hitchhiker hoaxes perpetrated by pranksters.

Goss's most dramatic moment during this research came when he interviewed a young Englishman who claimed that some months earlier he had given a ride to a silent young man who entered the car by opening the door, spoke not a word, indicated the direction he was traveling by merely pointing, and then disappeared while the car was in motion. This is certainly not a vanishing hitchhiker *legend,* but it does provide the heart of the story as the firsthand experience of a credible wit-

---

*Wellingborough, Northamptonshire: Aquarian Press, published in conjunction with ASSAP, the Association for the Scientific Study of Anomalous Phenomena.

ness, though whether the experience was imagined, dreamed, or real is impossible to say. Michael Goss himself reserved judgment on this and the other handful of authentic-sounding cases, suggesting only the hypothesis that perhaps all such "experiences" could be credited to the widespread knowledge of the folk legend, plus what he called "the romance of the open road," combining in some drivers' minds to create a hallucination that they themselves had personally met the phantom hitchhiker of folklore.

"The Decapitated Pet or Person"

The Pet Version: *The beloved family pet—a beautiful collie—loves to ride in the car with its head out the window, tongue dangling, and coat ruffled by the wind. [It can just as well be a beagle or a Labrador with its ears flapping, etc.]*

But a passing car comes too close and neatly clips the dog's head off; the car continues on several miles before anyone notices what has happened.

Known on both sides of the Atlantic, and often told by parents to children while admonishing them to keep their own heads, hands, and feet *inside* the car—"Do you hear me, *inside,* or I'm not driving another inch!" The human version of this story, however, I have encountered (so far) only in England:

A truckload of thin steel sheets is being driven along a highway in an industrial part of the Midlands. A man on a motorcycle with a sidecar drives up behind the load, and seeing no oncoming traffic, prepares to pass. But just as the motorcycle comes even with the truck, one of the steel sheets—not having been firmly secured—slides loose and flies straight out sideways towards the motorcycle, carried very swiftly by the wind from the speeding truck.

The motorcyclist is neatly decapitated by the steel sheet, and the headless corpse's grip convulsively tightens on the hand throttle, so that the cycle overtakes the truck. The sidecar keeps the cycle upright. When he sees the headless cyclist, the truck driver is so horrified that he suffers a heart attack, slumps over the steering wheel, and thus guides the truck straight into a line of people waiting at the side of the highway for a bus.

In June 1982 I was in England attending a conference on modern legends at the University of Sheffield, and among the urban legends we discussed was "The Decapitated Motorcyclist." One day the group took an arranged bus tour to York, and on the motorway a large "lorry" loaded with thin steel sheets passed our bus. Our bus driver then turned his head partly around and told us in all seriousness, "Very dangerous, that kind of load, very. Just last year a sheet of steel from a load like that came loose and cut a motorcyclist's head right off!" The driver seemed a bit taken aback by the laughter that greeted his grim comment.

♣"The Killer in the Backseat"

PHOENIX (UPI)—*As the woman walked to her car in a parking lot, she noticed a man following her.*

She jumped in her car and tore off, only to notice to her dismay that the man was following her in his car.

The woman drove through downtown Phoenix trying to elude him, passing stores, houses and bars. When that failed, she drove across town to the home of her brother-in-law, a policeman.

Horn honking, she pulled up and her brother-in-law came running out. She explained a man was following her and "There he is, right there!"

The policeman ran up to the man's car and demanded to know what he was doing.

"Take it easy. All I wanted to do was tell her about the guy in her back seat," the man said.

And indeed, there was a man huddled in the woman's back seat.

This true incident of several years ago . . .

This is the opening of a news story in the Flagstaff, Arizona, *Sun* for 17 July 1980 (p. 7), headlined "Police Officer Says Common Sense May Prevent Assault." The article continues by describing how a Phoenix police public information officer uses this and similar true-life anecdotes to teach citizens various crime prevention techniques. (See chapter 6 for other crime legends.)

In typical urban-legend fashion, the Phoenix story is completely plausible, and may well be based on an actual case. But it has the coloring of a widespread modern fable about it in the switcheroo ending in which the supposed assailant turns out to be the woman's rescuer. Usually the man crouched in back has a knife, hatchet, or meat cleaver clutched in his hand, ready to attack. If the incident is said to have taken place at night, the woman may notice the pursuing car because its headlights keep flashing from brights to the low beam; later the pursuer explains why, as in this conclusion to a retelling in which there are *two* rescuers who simply keep their brights on, in Cheryl Herbert's book of "true stories that will please any youngster" titled *Night Chase* (Nashville, Tennessee: Southern Publishing Company, 1977):

"We stayed right behind you and kept our bright lights in your window so that man wouldn't get up," Bob answered. *"We thought he would be afraid to be seen if the light was bright in your car."*

The common variation of the story has the lone woman driver pull into an all-night gas station for a fill-up and offer the attendant either a credit card or a large bill in payment. The attendant scrutinizes the card or the cash closely and then insists that there is something wrong with it that he is obliged to report. He convinces the woman to get out of her car and go into the station with him so he can call his boss (the credit office, the bank, etc.) and have her explain where she might have gotten the outdated/counterfeit/whatever item. Once inside, he locks the door, dials up the police, and explains to her that he spotted you-know-who again lurking in the backseat while he was pumping the gas. Our hero!

Collections and studies, from 1968 and 1969, of both major variations of "The Killer in the Backseat" are cited in *The Vanishing Hitchhiker.* A text—complete with a stated moral—quoted from a California reader in a 1982 Ann Landers column is reprinted in *The Choking Dober-man.*

"The Gerbil- (or Snake-) Caused Accident"

*A woman who has a gerbil in a cage on the front
seat of her car is driving across the Golden Gate
Bridge when the animal gets out of the cage and
climbs into her blouse. She immediately pulls over,
stops the car, jumps out, and begins to flail her arms
hysterically, trying to extract the gerbil.*

*Another motorist sees her contortions and assumes
she is grabbing at herself wildly because she is having
an epileptic seizure. In order to keep her from being
hit by other cars whizzing by, or from falling off the
bridge, he quickly pulls over, jumps out of his car,
and tries to wrestle her to the ground in a noble but
misguided effort to save her life.*

*Then a third driver, also male, passes by. He too
stops, believing that the first man is accosting her; he
jumps out of his car, strikes the first man in the face,
breaking his jaw and knocking him out.*

Reminded of other such legends about "Hilarious Accidents," as I have termed them in my writings, Professor
of Archaeology Karl M. Petruso of Boston University
sent me this one. He explains: "It was told to me by a
woman who was an accident investigator for an insurance firm in California. She described it as a case study
and a problem that was set for her class for an exam, the
purpose of which was to see if the students could work
out legal liabilities in the situation."

I sent a copy of the story to Professor Marc Galanter
of the University of Wisconsin–Madison Law School,
who has studied aspects of legal tradition and stereotyp-
ing in both folk and popular culture. (See "Legal Horror

Stories" in chapter 7.) He responded: "This is an instance of a genre that is intimately familiar to me. . . . It is very common for law professors to make up such stories (or elaborate and combine those they find in published cases) and use them for examinations. The student is given two or three hours to sort out the various issues in the case and write an answer."

We would seem to have here, then, merely some individual's retelling of a classroom example as a legend; but what about this next variation that arrived in a letter from Lynn Marler of Chico, California, just a week after Professor Galanter's:

In the late sixties a friend read to me over the phone the following story out of a San Francisco Bay Area newspaper: A woman got in her car to drive somewhere one day, and before she had gotten very far from home, felt something tickling her ankle. She looked down and saw a snake sticking out of the bottom of her pants leg.

The woman screamed, slammed on the brakes, skidded to a stop at the side of the road, and threw herself out of the car. She lay on the ground screaming in revulsion and kicking her legs about in an effort to dislodge the snake since she couldn't bring herself to touch it. A man driving by saw her and thought, "Oh, my God, that poor lady is having a seizure or something!" He stopped and ran over to her to try to find out what was wrong.

Another man driving by saw the first man bending over this kicking, screaming woman and thought, "Oh, no! That guy's attacking that woman!" He stopped, ran over, and punched the first man in the face. And all of that happened because of a harmless little garter snake.

Perhaps there's some validation of these as authentic modern folklore in one further hilarious car/animal/man/woman accident story given in Don Bishoff's column in the *Register-Guard* of Eugene, Oregon, on 22 October 1984. Bishoff says he got it from an acquaintance named Jim Bryant, and I am indebted to folklorist Sharon Sherman of the University of Oregon for sending me the clipping:

This story has a guy driving down the street, passing a car that has just come around the corner from the opposite direction. The woman driver in the other car shouts "Pig!" at the guy, who promptly retorts, "You're not so great-looking yourself!" Then he turns the corner—and runs over a pig in the street."

"The Nut and the Tire Nuts"

*A woman driving by herself at night has a flat tire
in front of the Oregon State Hospital at Pendleton.
She gets out of the car and begins to change the tire
but notices lurking not far away a shadowy figure she
presumes to be an inmate of the hospital. She is
frightened but continues to change the flat tire.*

*She removes the four lug nuts from the tire and
puts them in the hubcap, but in her haste she
accidentally stumbles over the hubcap and sends the
lug nuts flying into the darkness of the weeds and
rocks beside the road. They are lost.*

*Now she is terrified, and she notices the stranger
approaching her. He speaks . . . and offers her a
solution: take one lug nut from each of the three
other wheels and put it on the spare. She does, and
makes it safely to town.*

(Told to me by Salem, Oregon, *Statesman-Journal*
writer Tom Forstrom and photographer David Nuss during an interview in Portland on 10 July 1984.)

Forstrom included this same narrative in his story
"Urban Legends" in the *Statesman-Journal* on 26 July,
headlined "Oregon's own legend." A Salem reader,
John C. Bunnell, wrote to the editor a few days later to
point out that the same problem was set out in a story
by Martin Gardner in that month's issue of the magazine
Issac Asimov's Science Fiction. Gardner includes it in a short
story titled "The Road to Mandalay," in which the talking computer guiding a futuristic automobile going 200
km an hour down a twenty-lane freeway poses various

logic puzzles for the "driver" to solve. One of the car's brain teasers is the tire nut dilemma, but without the intervention of an outside person providing the solution. Certainly this is a traditional puzzle story that Gardner simply incorporated into his piece of science fiction. In oral circulation the plot is told either as a legend about a particular asylum or as a joke with the inmate's punchline, "I may be crazy, but I'm not stupid." In this form the story appears in Jeremy Leven's novel *Satan: His Psychotherapy and Cure by the Unfortunate Dr. Kassler, J.S.P.S.* (New York: Ballantine, 1983, p. 176). And as a classroom exercise the same puzzle is posed in Stewart L. Tubbs's *A Systems Approach to Small Group Interaction* (Reading, Massachusetts: Addison-Wesley Publishing, 2nd. ed., 1984, p. 343).

A similar story sometimes encountered both orally and in print concerns a large truck that becomes stuck in a highway underpass. The vehicle is within an inch of clearing the space but cannot be budged either forward or backward—until a small child watching the situation suggests that some air be let out of each of the truck's tires. When this is done, the truck is lowered enough to make it through. Martin Gardner also presents this one as a logic puzzle in his *Perplexing Puzzles and Tantalizing Teasers* (New York: Archway Paperbacks, Pocket Books, 1971, p. 70).

≯"The Severed Fingers" (An Australian Version)

*My brother Alan tells me about a young man who
owned a Volkswagen "beetle" car, who took his girl
friend to a drive-in movie. During the performance
four young men in an old Falcon next to them, who
were drinking heavily, were using shocking language
loudly while discussing the story line of the picture.
The young man remonstrated with them, at their use
of bad language in the presence of his lady friend, to
be met with torrents of abuse.*

*When the show was over, these louts all got out of
their car and advanced on him. He hastily wound up
the windows of his car, started the engine, and locked
the doors. He was about to drive off, when three of
the young men lifted the back of his car into the air,
thereby robbing the wheels of traction, while the
fourth tried to force the door open.*

*The young man panicked, engaged low gear, and
revved the motor. Eventually the weight of the car
proved too much, it was dropped to the ground, and
the spinning wheels carried it off with a tremendous
jerk, leaving the larrikins behind. When the young
man got home he found three bloody fingers jammed
behind the rear bumper.*

(This text is in the words of Bill Scott, quoted from his
Complete Book of Australian Folklore [Sydney: Ure Smith,
1976], p. 368.)

I mention English versions of "The Severed Fingers"
traceable to the early 1960s in *The Choking Doberman* and

show that variations of the story are found elsewhere in Europe and in the United States. All of the modern car stories about torn-off fingers seem to go back to a much earlier legend in which the hand of a would-be robber is cut off while he is in the act of grasping a horseman's bridle trying to stop him. See my earlier book for a French text from 1579. The relationship of "The Severed Fingers" to other traditional and modern legends is represented by the box labeled "Fingers Severed in Vehicle Crime" in the diagram on p. 46 of the present book.

"Old vs. Young"

My bartender told me this one; she says that it is a true story. An older woman drives her Mercedes into a crowded parking lot. After searching in vain for a parking space she spies another car getting ready to leave, so she pulls up nearby and waits. But just as the other car pulls out a shiny blue sports car zips into the space. The young driver smiles as he gets out and shouts, "You've got to be young and fast!" The woman thinks about this a moment, then rams the sports car. She backs up and rams it again and again. The young man comes running in horror. "What are you doing?" he shouts. The woman smiles and says, "You've got to be old and rich." Then she drives away.

(Received via computer on "seismo net," dated 10 March 1985. Many jokes, legends, and personal experience stories circulate in similar electronic form nowadays.)

The model and make of the rich woman's car vary in this popular current story, and sometimes she hands the young man her insurance agent's business card before she drives away. She may comment, "I'm just older and richer than you are." Peter Kiddle of Halwell, Devon, England, sent me a version heard in Torquay "at the height of the tourist season." Here an old man is being very careful about parking his Rolls Royce—pulling out to re-park carefully between the lines—when two lads from Birmingham beat him out of the parking spot in their beat-up minicar. He crushes their car against a wall and delivers the usual punchline.

3

Horrors

✒ "The Clever Baby-sitter"

Two teenage girls are overheard talking on a bus or subway about their baby-sitting jobs. They are comparing notes on various problems they have had handling kids, and they are sharing tricks of the trade. One asks the other what she does about crying babies: "How in the world can you stop them from crying once they start?"

"Oh, that's no problem," the second girl answers. "I just turn on the gas in the oven and hold the baby's head inside until it falls asleep."

In *The Choking Doberman* I quote versions of this story from the 1950s up to the 1980s and ranging geographically from New York City to Florida, "down South," and Denver. Sometimes the baby-sitter uses a stove-top gas burner as a pacifier; in either case, the story is often given as a warning against leaving children with unknown guardians.

Lately I have had references to "The Clever Baby-sitter" sent to me from Maryland, Illinois, Arizona, and California; these extend back in people's memories to the late 1920s and 1930s. The older datings are sup-

ported by the relatively more common use of gas cooking ovens in the past than now, as well as by the fact that
sometimes it is the maids of wealthy people who were
supposedly overheard discussing child care. Usually the
event is said to have taken place on a specific trolley, bus,
or subway line that the friend of a friend who is attributed with the information rides to work daily. One
correspondent remembers a lecturer in English literature at a British university mentioning that in the nine-
teenth century both laudanum (an opium derivative) and
coal gas were used as tranquilizers for restive babies.

"The War Profiteer"

*The period is sometime during World War II. The
scene is a bus or subway in a large American city.
Two women are talking about how well their
husbands are doing as manufacturers of war supplies.
"We have plenty of money," one of them is saying,
"two cars, and a ready market for everything our
plants can make. I wish the war would go on forever."
This is too much for another passenger, a man who
rises from his seat, walks over to the women, and
slaps the speaker hard across the face. "That's for my
son who is a marine fighting in the South Pacific
[killed in Europe, etc.]," he says.*

Variously reported, but never verified by a firsthand
participant or witness, this story represents both what we
think may be true about war profiteers and how we personally imagine ourselves rebuking one of them.

"The Mother's Threat Carried Out"

The most horrible tale I remember concerned "the little boy who wet." Depending on the version, he was two or three years old. Despite scoldings, he resisted toilet training until his exasperated mother warned: "If you don't learn, I'm going to cut it off."

Unfortunately, she was overheard by the boy's older sister. So one day, when the children's mother was away, the boy wet again, and the girl took up a pair of shears and cut it off. He almost bled to death."

This text was sent to me by Edward H. Eulenberg, a former newspaper reporter in Chicago, who added, "This yarn circulated among middle-aged ladies of my mother's generation, with all sorts of variations. It was so bizarre that I never pursued it, and I never saw it in print."

My own pursuit of this story—which I've also heard in several versions—led to the following printed example describing a *double* tragedy, as found in Rodney Dale's entertaining collection of British urban legends *The Tumour in the Whale* (London: Duckworth, 1978), pp. 151–52:

There is a another harassed mum with two children —the small boy and the larger girl. This time, she shouts: "If you don't go to sleep I'll . . . I'll . . . cut off your willie." This threat seems to work, so she goes downstairs and relaxes with a suitable glass. Then there is a scream from withup, and she rushes to the foot of the stairs to be greeted with her angelic daughter, brandishing a pair of dressmaking scissors, saying: "He didn't keep quiet, so I cut it off for you."

To the hospital quickly! Mum grabs him from the cot, wraps him in a blanket and rushes down stairs, shouting to her daughter: "You'd better come with me so that I can keep an eye on you." She runs out to the garage, opens the doors and lays her son on the backseat. Then she climbs in, reverses out of the garage, and runs over her daughter.

Dale's previous example of "The Mother's Threat," alluded to above, is set on an overnight ferry to Ireland. Baby keeps crying, refusing to quiet down and go to sleep, until the mother shouts, "If you don't shut up, I'll put you out of the porthole." Finally the two children get settled, and mother goes up for some supper; but when she returns, the baby is gone, the porthole is open, and the daughter is peacefully asleep.

Rodney Dale repeats both versions in his book *It's True, It Happened to a Friend* (London: Duckworth, 1984, pp. 90–91), a collection that contains a number of old favorites like "The Choking Doberman," "The Hairy-Armed Hitchhiker," and "The Turkey Neck."

"The Cabbage Patch Tragedy"

*What happens to your Cabbage Patch Doll when it
bites the dust? A San Francisco woman found out
when she sent a broken doll back to the
manufacturer. She expected a replacement. What she
got instead was . . . a death certificate and a letter of
condolence.*

(Item in the "Signs of the Times" column in the *River-
front News* of St. Louis, Missouri, December 12–18,
1984.)

This one had been neatly debunked in a Thanksgiving
Day, 1984, column by *St. Louis Post-Dispatch* writer Elaine
Viets, but apparently to no avail on the local scene, as the
above item shows. Viets's story had begun, "Be thankful
you aren't the public relations person for the Cabbage
Patch dolls." Also, as she explained, be aware that at
BabyLand General Hospital in Cleveland, Georgia,
where the Xavier Roberts's soft sculpture originals are
produced, they're always called "kids," not "dolls."

You *adopt*, not merely *buy*, a Cabbage Patch Kid—
whether an original or the Coleco Industries mass-pro-
duced version that swept madness into the doll market
for the Christmases of 1983 and 1984. Either version of
the doll—uh, kid—comes with adoption papers, but only
the BabyLand General version is also registered in the
"hospital" computer. There are no death certificates—
either way.

Nevertheless, the claim that death certificates have
been issued for burned, "dead," imitation, or defective
Cabbage Patchers has swept the country, keeping pace

with the mania for the toys themselves. Variations include that the doll is returned in a little coffin for burial, that the owner is billed for a funeral, or that a citation is issued for child abuse. People have written me from all over asking if stories like this that they heard from a friend of a friend were true. I say No, of course, and so does Elaine Viets, who quotes Mari Forquer in the Cabbage Patch public relations department in Georgia. Forquer is quoted as sighing, "Has that story surfaced again? I thought we buried it. No pun intended."

But the death story remains, so to speak, alive and well. For instance, Bob Talbert's "Notebag" in the *Detroit Free Press* headlines a column (15 February 1985), "Let's bury this Cabbage Patch death tale." The way *he* heard it, a doll disintegrated when Mom tossed it into the washing machine for a bath. "Pure fiction, folks" opines Talbert, and he's right. Yet on 30 September 1985 the legend appeared in the London *Daily Telegraph* in the "London Day by Day" column, along with the information that a Canadian dentist was said to be fixing Cabbage Patch Kids' teeth for $10.

There *are,* however, really summer camps for Cabbage Patch Kids, in case you were wondering if that one could be true. But as the BabyLand spokeswoman says, "This is not an endorsed activity."

Medical Horrors

The fear of undesirable foreign matter or loathsome creatures getting at or even *into* our bodies—along with the attendant fear of the medical procedures necessary to remove said contaminants—has spawned several horror legends. These include the stories about spiders in hairdos and ants in sinuses discussed in *The Vanishing Hitchhiker* as well as the legends of snake-infested people and misplaced cadavers included in *The Choking Doberman*. Here are three further such stories, involving medical problems, really yucky ones, that have gone around lately.

1. "The Spider Bite"

A young woman from the Midwest is on vacation in Florida, enjoying some long, lazy afternoons basking on the beach. [Of course, she may just as well be a young woman from Anywhere, USA—or even from England, Germany, or Scandinavia—vacationing in Mexico, South America, Spain, or Africa. In every instance, the same horrible thing happens to her.]

She falls asleep on the beach one day, and a spider creeps up beside her and bites her on the cheek (or forehead), leaving a small sore that soon enlarges to a great big ugly boil. When she gets back home and the bite fails to heal, but indeed grows even larger and more awful, she consults a doctor; he lances the boil, and dozens of tiny spiders rush out. The beach spider had evidently laid eggs under her skin.

The young woman is so horrified that she either

has a heart attack or must undergo psychiatric treatment.

This story has been popular in both American and European folklore for some twenty years. Sometimes it is asserted that the woman had a small open sore on her face even before the vacation, or that when the doctor must postpone an appointment to have the boil lanced she is in such pain and depression that she involuntarily scratches it open, thus releasing the baby spiders herself. A version of this latter form of the legend enlarged to a short story is the title piece in *The Bite and Other Apocryphal Tales* by Francis Grieg (London: Jonathan Cape, 1981; published in the United States as *Heads You Lose . . .* (New York: Crown, 1982). "Grieg" (a pseudonym) has the woman have her boil pop open spontaneously to release the spiders in the hot water of her bath. I've heard one version in which the bite occurs on a jet plane returning tourists from North Africa to London; the woman quickly brushes away the creature, which came out of the plane's upholstery, but its eggs had already been laid in her body.

Fear of insects and spiders, along with distrust of other nations (particularly those more southern than one's own), are standard features of several other urban legends, including a recent story about South American screw worms being snorted up the nose from a bad batch of cocaine.

2. "The Hair Ball"

Great uncle so-and-so, a barber, died in some sort of unusual circumstances that required an investigation to be done to determine the cause of death. An autopsy revealed large hair balls in his lungs; supposedly these had formed from all the bits of hair that he had breathed in during his years of work. The hair had rolled around and around with the action of his breathing until they became large enough to suffocate him.

[And there was also the little girl who always chewed on the ends of her braids. She too died of a huge hair ball, but this time one that was lodged in her stomach.]

3. "The Colo-Rectal Mouse"

This is only the most recent of many legends about things that people—often homosexuals—have supposedly put inside a body orifice and then come to an emergency room to have removed. Emergency-room personnel often tell these tales, but always about someone else's hospital or someone else's shift.

A homosexual guy has had a friend of his use a greased plastic tube to insert a mouse or other small animal into his rectum, since he has heard that this is the ultimate thrill. It may be a gerbil or small lizard, and its tail may break off when they try to remove it themselves. Sometimes the gay guy simply comes in for help in removing a stuck object, which then proves to be a mouse skeleton. Cages for pet gerbils and the like often have small plastic tubes in them intended as runways for the animals, so this is what suggested trying the act in the first place.

"The Colo-Rectal Mouse" sounds a bit like a homosexual version of "The Stuck Couple," and it is becoming almost as well known as that earlier legend. In Fall 1984 I heard five versions of this story from places as scattered as Pennsylvania, through the Midwest, Colorado, Utah, and southern California. Correspondents—particularly from New York and California—have continued to mention the story through 1985. In one recent variation ("gerbiling") it is said that the gerbil is first put into a plastic bag and given a shot of laughing gas to pep it up a little.

"I Believe in Mary Worth"

WHO KNOWS?

*Who was Mary Worth? Not the comic strip Mary
Worth, but the scary Mary Worth. If you're over
thirty, you probably haven't heard of her, but
everyone younger seems to be familiar with the game.
It's usually played at parties or summer camps. People
gather in a dark room, stare into a mirror, and repeat
some variation of "I do believe in Mary Worth" a
certain number of times (10, 47, 50, 100). This results
in Mary Worth appearing in the mirror or scratching
the person repeating the litany.*

*The patron who asked this question thought Mary
Worth was a witch who was executed and buried near
Wadsworth, Illinois. He wanted to know who she was
and exactly where she was buried. Roger Sutton,
Zion-Benton librarian, says she is not local. He grew
up in the Boston area and knew about her. Local
tradition there said she was buried in Quincy,
Massachusetts. Roger also went to school in
California, and people there also knew the game.*

*We've talked to many people about this. No one
has any background information on the game. Was
Mary a real person? Where did this originate? Is there
any connection to the comic strip? . . . Can anyone
add anything to the Mary Worth legend?*

(The above was published in *Nexus,* newsletter of the
Chicago North Suburban Library System's Reference
Service in Spring 1983, and sent to me by Mary Frances
Burns, Head of the Reference Department of the Pala-

tine [Illinois] Public Library District. Boy—the stuff librarians are supposed to know!)

The person who *does* know something—though not *all* the answers, which no one seems to have—about Mary Worth, alias Mary Worthington, Mary Whales, Mary Johnson, Bloody Mary, Mary Lou, or Mary Jane, is folklorist Janet Langlois, whose essay " 'Mary Whales, I Believe in You': Myth and Ritual Subdued" appeared in the journal *Indiana Folklore* (vol. 11, 1978, pp. 5–33) and was reprinted in *Indiana Folklore: A Reader*, edited by Linda Dégh (Bloomington: Indiana University Press, 1980; pp. 196–224). Langlois initially heard the story of Mary (the "myth" of her title) told by a twelve-year-old student from a Catholic school for black children in Indianapolis who gave her a rudimentary description of the litany of calling up her spirit (the "ritual"). Visiting the school to interview eighty of the girl's schoolmates, Langlois collected seventeen versions of the legend/game, providing a good cross-section of material that is evidently known all over the country.

The "Mary Worth," let us call her, of the legends is generally said to have been killed in a local automobile accident in which her face was severely mutilated. Her spirit may be seen hitchhiking, but it disappears before she reaches the end of the ride (does that sound familiar?). In what Langlois dubs a "double inverse relationship," the Mary Worth of the game or ritual reappears as a result of the participant's actions, and she tries to scratch them on the face. In a sense, then, she emerges out of the participant's own reflection, which should give Freudians something to chew on.

Mary and Herbert Knapp give essentially the same description of how to summon Mary as a bit of general American childlore in their book *One Potato, Two Potato:*

The Secret Education of American Children (New York: W. W. Norton, 1976, p. 242) with the elaboration that she "comes at you with a knife in her hand and a wart on her nose." Another account of the ritual is titled "A Ghost in the Mirror" in Alvin Schwartz's *More Scary Stories to Tell in the Dark* (New York: Lippincott, 1984, pp. 58–59), which picks up Langlois's theory that the Mary Worth game may be related to the famous Chicano legend of "La Llorona," the weeping woman whose ghost is said to wander eternally, searching for her own children whom she has murdered.

Not nice stuff, this; so what does it all have to do with the kindly Mary Worth of the comics? Nothing, as far as I can tell, except for sharing the same name, a feature that was probably brought about by simple substitution of something that was familiar and sounded right. Ghost-lore, mirrorlore, witchlore, and brought-it-on-yourself lore is all very old in world folk tradition, so the precise origin of "I Believe in Mary Worth" cannot be determined. But the combining of several old motifs into a modern localized story is a familiar process, and that seems to be what happened here.

Unfortunately, this isn't the sort of answer that library patrons like to get—or librarians like to give. So I welcome other versions and further theories. As the Knapps phrase it, we would really like to know *why* Mary Worth, "the respectable busybody" in the comic strips, seems to be "moonlighting as a mirror witch."

4

Contaminations

"The Spider in the Yucca"

Fear not, if you have a yucca plant from Marks and Spencer. It won't have a tarantula in the pot. Lots of people recently have been afraid that they will find deadly spiders in their yuccas. They have bombarded newspapers with complaints: they have bombarded M & S stores around the country with demands for action. No one quite knows why.

The story, as told to newspapers, is always the same. A friend (for it is inevitably a friend) hears a mysterious squeaking noise coming from her M & S yucca. He or she rings M & S, who tell him/her to stay away from it while they rush a van round to pick it up, which they do.

Every time the story was checked out by M & S, it was found to be untrue. Head office grew concerned at the huge apocryphal tidal wave that was hitting them and after investigation, claim that it is, in any case, virtually impossible since the yuccas are imported from Africa via Holland, where they are re-planted and potted. "We've been literally inundated with calls" said an M & S spokesman, "but not one spider has yet been spotted."

(Clipped from the "Diary" column in the *Guardian* for 19 April 1985 by Mat Coward of London and sent to me.)

See chapter 5, "A Snake Story," for a legend that similarly begins with a scary beast brought into a home in a large potted plant.

"The Unlucky Contacts"

A couple on their first date become very well acquainted; they are highly attracted to each other, and decide to spend the night together in her apartment. Having had a bit too much to drink, they soon collapse into bed and fall into a deep sleep. But the man wakes up during the night with a powerfully dry throat; luckily there is a glass full of water right there on the night table, which he downs in one gulp. The next morning as his woman friend slowly awakens, she seems to be fumbling around the night table for something. "What is it, honey?" he inquires solicitously. She continues to grope around half-blindly, muttering, "Where the heck's that water glass I always leave my contact lenses in overnight?"

This one is sometimes told on a prominent person, such as a congressman, who spends the night with a prostitute. In any version it combines the double fears about ingesting the wrong thing (like tapeworms in the miracle diet pills) and the generalized suspicion about the comfort and safety of contact lenses. The fact that many contact wearers like to tell favorite personal anecdotes about loss of their lenses affords this story greater credibility. Syndicated columnist Mike Royko of the *Chicago Tribune* in a column on the hazards of contact lenses that was distributed to newspapers on November 2, 1985, had this recollection: "We've all heard the stories about people who awake really thirsty during the night and, in reaching for a glass of water on the night stand, accidentally drink their contact lenses."

For another recent legend about contacts, see chapter 7,

in which a horrendous story about the lenses becoming permanently fused to a person's cornea as a result of a welding accident is related—and, of course, debunked. The following story is a variation on the theme of the personal health aid becoming lost.

.

"The Wrong Teeth"
(An Australian version)

There is the story of the husband who was always trying to score off his wife. This went on for years, until both were middle-aged people. Then on one weekend they went to the beach with friends for the day. This story is usually told about the Gold Coast in Queensland or Bondi Beach in Sydney. At any rate, husband was a keen surfer still, and he persuaded his wife to go swimming with him despite the big surf running this particular day. The inevitable happened, and his wife was caught by a dumper and rolled helplessly up the beach. In the process she opened her mouth to shout, and lost her false teeth, much to her dismay. Her husband went ostensibly to help her find the missing dentures, along with their friends who accompanied them on the excursion, and, winking hugely at them, he slipped his own false teeth out and then pretended to find them. He offered them to his wife, who rinsed them in the sea and then tried to fit them in. They would not fit, of course, and to the husband's horror she flung them far out into the breaking waves, saying, "It's no good, those aren't mine!"

(Another text from Bill Scott's *Complete Book of Australian Folklore,* p. 369; see the reference under "The Severed Fingers" in chapter 2. This and other Australian versions of urban legends are in Scott's book *The Long and the Short and the Tall* [Sydney: Western Plains Publishers, 1985, pp. 223–251].)

Scott adds a variation of the story set on a fishing trip. An angler loses his false teeth while seasick, and when another man offers his own teeth as a joke, the first angler, not realizing this, throws them away into the sea.

✹"The Stolen Specimen"

A friend of a friend has had some unusual pains lately and suspects that she may have contracted a urinary infection. She calls her doctor for an appointment to have a checkup. The doctor instructs her to bring in the first urine specimen she can collect the next morning and to come at 9 o'clock. In the morning, however, the only small closed bottle she can find is a minibottle—the souvenir of a recent plane trip. Well, what the heck, it's the contents that counts, not the container.

Driving to the doctor's office, the woman stops briefly at a convenience store to pick up the morning paper. She leaves her specimen lying in the front seat of the car. And as she exits the store with her paper she sees a man reach quickly into her car, snatch the minibottle, and run.

Variations of this legend say that the specimen was stolen from a diabetic or from a pregnant woman similarly required to bring in specimens. In the latter instance, the scenario is that the friend of a friend was supposed to have observed the pregnant woman in a store parking lot hunched over the wheel of her car shaking. When the bystander asks if she needs help, she replies, "Oh, no, I'm only laughing at what just happened to me!" Sometimes the patient has been asked to save twenty-four hours' worth of urine (good grief!) but has only an empty whiskey or wine bottle on hand for the purpose. In English versions of the story the bottle may be lifted from the patient riding on a subway or bus, or else the patient has it in a bicycle basket while on the way to the doctor's office. There are also what I call solid-food variants of the story in which a dog owner taking Rover for a walk neatly cleans up the pet's droppings and carries them for disposal in a paper bag; but someone snatches the bag.

All these variations are really only a set of changes rung upon the old dead-cat-in-the-package plot, for which see chapter 1. The use of urine in diagnosis also recalls the venerable prank of a medical instructor pretending to test urine for sugar content by dipping his finger into a specimen and tasting it. Having got most of his class to try the experiment, the instructor then demonstrates more slowly how he switches fingers between the specimen and his tongue.

The Poinsettia Myth

Don't ever let your kids eat the poinsettias! They are deadly poisonous, and every year several poor unsuspecting little ones are killed at Christmastime by taking just the slightest nibble from a poinsettia plant. There oughta be a law!

The reason there is no law is that this simply is not true. My thanks to Joan Jackson, Garden Editor of the *San Jose Mercury News,* for pointing out to me the prevalence of this fallacy. She writes, "Every year at Christmas I can expect to see at least one wire story coming along that says, be careful—don't let your kids eat the poinsettia or it will poison them." A fact sheet prepared by Ecke Poinsettia Growers offers these assurances:

Origin: *The poinsettia poison myth had its origin in 1919 when a two-year-old child of an Army officer stationed in Hawaii died of poisoning, and the cause was incorrectly assumed to be a poinsettia leaf.*

Tests come up clean: *Research conducted at Ohio State University determined that the poinsettia plant is not toxic. Results of this project published in 1971 concluded that the poinsettia is not harmful to either people or animals. The U. S. Department of Agriculture reports that while certain popular houseplants can be toxic, and some are actually poisonous, the poinsettia is absolutely harmless.*

Impressive track record: *The Poison Control Center of the Food and Drug Administration monitors information from 500 reporting Centers in 50 states. The Center reports that to their knowledge, no one has ever been known to be hospitalized or treated for poisoning as the result of ingesting any part of the poinsettia plant.*

Government clearance: *The U. S. Consumer Products Safety Commission determined that the poinsettia should not be required to carry a "warning label" in a statement issued December 19, 1975. This recommendation was based on their investigation in which no evidence was found to support the poinsettia poison myth. The Commission did suggest, however, that the poinsettia should be considered a non-food substance which if eaten could cause some discomfort.*

Mere discomfort, however, is not the stuff of legend. It's gotta be death or nothing. But my advice still is, "Please don't eat the poinsettias!"

"The Secret Ingredient"
(As heard on the radio)

My friends, what I am about to tell you is so horrifying that it can hardly be believed, but I'm convinced that it is true, and I'm obliged to share my findings with all you good Christians out there in radioland so you can join me in fighting a diabolical scheme that exists right in our midst. But—as I said— it is so horrible, so bloodthirsty, so damnably despicable that you may not believe it at first, any more than I did.

Would you believe it if I told you that many of the cosmetics you use every day contain an ingredient derived from the fetuses of aborted babies!? This is no mere guess or rumor, but a well-established fact supported by hundreds of pages of documented research. This secret youth-preserving ingredient is called "collagen," and technically it is just the gelatinous substance found in all animal connective tissues. The traditional industrial source of collagen has been animals—usually beef byproducts—but lately many big international companies have found a ready source of high-quality collagen closer at hand—in the abortion clinics and hospitals of our "great land" and in foreign countries where millions of fetuses are killed and disposed of every year. From these murdered babies fiendish companies are deriving the collagens now used in more than seventy-five percent of the beauty products sold today.

Be sure to check all of your own cosmetics, shampoos, etc.! Unless the label says "animal"

collagen or "bovine" collagen, you may be supporting
this damnable industry by using human byproducts
yourself! The very thought of such a thing should be
enough to make you drop to your knees and pray.
Rid your cosmetic shelf of all such products forever,
and boycott the manufacturers who are responsible
for them!

This is a fairly mild and generalized version of a scare
story that has been much talked about by fundamentalist
ministers on Christian radio stations and television
shows for the past several years. Often the claim is buttressed by reference to published studies and volumi-
nous documentation, copies of which will be sent to lis-
teners upon request and the payment of a handling fee.
Usually, too, statistics on the numbers of abortions performed in this country and abroad are given, along with
lurid descriptions of how the fetuses are supposedly
ground up in processing. As the story is repeated, some
people have altered it to describe collagens also used in
an expensive perfume, and a related rumor is that fetuses
are sealed in plastic for use as paperweights.

This "Secret Ingredient" claim is extremely ambiguous, since the term "collagen" by itself on a label implies
nothing beyond the standard protein substance produced by acceptable means from animal byproducts. A
company called The Collagen Corporation, for example,
founded in 1975, manufactures what the *New York Times*
described (27 March 1982, p. 29 of the Business Section)
as "a protein-based cream used primarily in cosmetic
surgery." It is marketed under the tradename "Zyderm"
and used for treating such skin problems as surgery scars
and acne. The product is derived, say the manufacturers,
"by treating cowhides with a proprietary process."

Such is probably the typical source and use of collagen

in health care, though it is also true that some cosmetic products, mainly foreign ones, do specify placentas as a human source of collagen. For example, the literature on Cellular Magic cosmetics distributed in 1983 by Cellular Cosmetic Laboratories of Houston, Texas, lists "human cellular tissue factors," "human placenta extract," and "human collagen" among their ingredients. But it's a long leap of imagination from a placenta-derived product to one made from aborted fetuses. So far, only the media ministers and their fans seem to have made that assumption.

To their credit, the Moral Majority has investigated and denounced the "Secret Ingredient" allegations, despite the belief in them by some of their members. In the July 1984 issue of *Moral Majority Report* (vol. 5, no. 7, p. 4), writer Roy C. Jones identifies a 1981 source of the rumor in a Washington columnist but reports that "extensive research" carried out since the original story appeared uncovered no evidence of fetal material being used in cosmetics.

It's possible that a lurid novel by Fred Mustard Stewart called *The Methuselah Enzyme* (New York: Arbor House, 1970) has fueled this story, though the word "collagen" itself appears nowhere in it. The setting of the novel is a youth-restoring clinic in Switzerland to which a trio of over-the-hill wealthy investors and their three younger and unaware friends repair. Part of the cure the old folks take is surreptitiously drawn from the pineal glands of their companions; the rest comes from fetuses aborted from local young women who have been artifically impregnated for the purpose. The whole nasty scheme in this piece of sensational fiction backfires when drastic side effects begin to appear.

Recently the Food & Drug Administration (FDA) of the Department of Health and Human Services has felt it necessary to warn hospitals and other health care organizations about the "Secret Ingredient" rumor. The following appeared in an FDA newsletter sent out in February 1985 from the Seattle office; it identifies other sources of the story:

ALLEGED USE OF FETUSES IN PRODUCTS DENIED

Pamphlets and letters to newspapers have recently alleged that human fetuses are used in the cosmetics industry. These allegations have been fed by the French book called "The Traffic in Unborn Babies" which claims that human fetuses are used as cosmetic ingredients.

A Vatican newspaper recently editorialized on the basis of the book. Similar allegations about cosmetics have circulated in pro-life circles in the U.S. since 1981, according to the July Moral Majority Report, but the same newspaper and its researchers have found no substantiation for the charges.

Nor has FDA. Regarding the cosmetics and other products FDA regulates, FDA does not believe the allegations are applicable to the United States, and is not aware they apply in Europe. The allegations may arise from misunderstanding of the following facts:

—Placenta, the after-birth of normal childbirth, is collected here and elsewhere for the substances it contains. These include plasma and other medically useful products. Some placenta may be used for the protein, or "collagen", in some cosmetics. Animals are another source of this substance. Collagen injected to remove thin lines on the face is derived from cows.

Because of earlier allegations, FDA inspectors were asked to look during inspections of cosmetic firms for indications of any use of human fetal material. The inspections have shown no use of fetuses or fetal tissue.

(I am endebted to David L. Webster IV, of Mercer Island, Washington, for sending me this and several other pieces of information he has collected about "The Secret Ingredient.")

In her column of Sunday 28 April 1985 Ann Landers published a letter from an Alabama reader who had "been told by three people that collagen is made from aborted babies. She added, "My sources are an evangelist, a beauty consultant and my neighbor who worked in a hospital." Ann replied, "There is not a shred of truth to that story. . . . [It's] unadulterated garbage." And for the concerned reader's further edification, Ann also explained that collagen was merely "hydrolyzed animal protein that comes from leftovers at the slaughterhouses." How'd you like to rub some of *that* on your face!

Another Ann Landers reader persisted in pursuing the matter, however, and on 15 July 1985, the first of her two columns devoted to Ann's personal investigation of "The Secret Ingredient" story appeared. In the first she declared, "Never in my 30 years of writing this column have I run into such half-baked distortions, complete lies and twisted facts contrived to make a story sound believable." (At least one newspaper carrying the column simply summed it up as "A grizzly story.") The next day's Ann Landers column looked into an alleged inhumane fetus experiment in Finland and found it to be benign, scientific, and well controlled. For good measure, then, Ann had checked with a group of leading doctors in large hospitals and university medical centers to find out exactly what *does* happen to aborted fetuses. Suffice it to say that the answers from medical officials revealed absolutely no connections whatever to the cosmetics industry. The collagen in beauty products come from what Ann called "slaughterhouse leftovers" or discarded human afterbirths, which I find grisly enough even without the grotesque legends.

✈"The Eaten Pets"

DOGGIE-QUE?

How would you like an invitation to a barbeque: the entree: roast loin of dog. Shocked? I hope so, because such barbeques are part of our society, here in Salt Lake City!

Many refugees have flocked to Utah from Vietnam, Laos, and Korea, and some of them bring with them native customs, one of these (a more abhorrent one) is the slaughtering and eating of a dog.

I was truly shocked to hear recently of a refugee family's birthday barbeque featuring a main course of dog that was formerly a family pet. In fact the Salt Lake City Animal Control said "It happens all the time." . . .

(Part of a letter in "The Public Forum" of *The Salt Lake Tribune,* 11 May 1984.)

DOG-EATERS DEBUNKED

Do not too easily accept the statement . . . that Asian refugees barbecue pet dogs here "all the time." Investigations in other communities of similar stories have generally debunked them.

For example, in 1980–81 rumors were flying in Stockton, CA, that Southeast Asian refugees were capturing and eating pets. Evidence was supposedly found in garbage cans, and people had heard about Vietnamese wanting to buy puppies or kittens to use for food. Some people said that cats' tails had been seen hanging over the side of a refugee family's cooking pot. But a folklorist from a local college studied the matter and found that none of the stories was true and that all alleged sources (such as garbage collection companies and city officials) denied them.

In February 1982 a writer for the Fairvax, VA, Journal *looked into similar local rumors; once again there were claims about pet remains found in garbage cans and refugees buying pets. Another story described bodies of small animals found in the Asians' freezers by police investigators. The officials supposedly involved called the stories "far-out," even though dozens of citizens claimed to have heard of documented instances of pet-eating.*

These examples of modern folklore are similar to earlier stories about pet remains found in garbage cans behind Chinese restaurants. Recently the influx of Oriental refugees aroused Americans' suspicions and the stories have been revived in new forms. This is one of the traditions I discuss in my book The Choking Doberman.

(Part of my reply to the above, published in "The Public Forum" on 31 May 1984.)

"Eaten Pet" rumors and legends take many forms. Sometimes, for instance, it is a pony bought by Tongans in the United States for a child's birthday party, except that the horse is intended for the meal rather than as a present for the child. Another common twist is the notion that there has been a recent rash of missing pets in the community; the statistics on such crimes, dug up by some enterprising reporter, usually prove to be normal. A switcheroo on the legend is "The Dog's Dinner," in which some Western tourists' pet is cooked and served to them in a Hong Kong restaurant because of a misunderstanding about who had ordered what in that party of three in the corner.

Two news stories in the Vancouver, B.C., *Sun* in mid-December 1985 describe police and SPCA investigation of an incident on 8 December involving "an immigrant family" found to be roasting a dog over an open fire in their basement. The East Vancouver family's origin was referred to only as "a culture where eating dogs is not considered wrong." It was concluded that cruelty-to-animals charges could not be brought, because the evidence —the cooked dog—did not show conclusively that the animal had suffered when being prepared for roasting. Officials asked to be contacted by any neighbors "who might recently have lost a dog," but no missing dogs were reported in the *Sun.* Likely, news reports of this kind lend credence to the rumors and legends about Asian immigrants stealing pets in order to eat them.

Evidently such stories are rather old, may have had some basis in fact, and have been directed at different targets in various times and places, as the following examples suggest:

ONE HUNDRED YEARS AGO [1885]

A woman named Ann Little, 54 years of age, was charged on Tuesday last at the Gateshead county police-court with stealing one game-cock and two cats, and was sentenced to three months' imprisonment. In the course of the evidence it was stated that for some time past the prisoner has been in the habit of stealing cats, skinning them, and selling them to her neighbours as Scotch hares. About a fortnight ago, information to this effect was given to the police; and on the prisoner's house being searched, the remains of several cats were found. In and about the house were discovered no less than forty cats' skins, some of which have been identified by neighbours as the remains of their favourites. When charged with the offence, the prisoner replied, "I have sold several, and we have eaten several ourselves; they are very like a rabbit when cooked."

(*British Medical Journal,* 12 January 1985, quoting *BMJ* 1885, i:393; sent to me by Dr. Martin C. Gregory of the Dialysis Training Center, University of Utah School of Medicine.)

An earlier English reference to this eaten pets story occurs in Charles Dickens's *Pickwick Papers* (1836–37, chapter 19) where Sam Weller tells Mr. Pickwick about some meat pies made from kittens by an unscrupulous pieman. This was pointed out by Jacqueline Simpson in "Urban Legends in *The Pickwick Papers," Journal of American Folklore* 96 (1983), pp. 462–70.

And here is part of an Australian variant in verse:

FROM "MY OTHER CHINEE COOK"

[The poem describes how a Chinese cook working for an Australian family, though considered "lazy," "cheeky," "dirty," and "sly," has the one virtue of making delectable rabbit pie. But when he is ordered to produce one more such meal after a full week of them, he at first shakes his head and then reveals his terrible secret.]

"Go, do as you are bid," I cried, "we wait for no
    reply;
Go! let us have tea early, and another rabbit-pie!"
Oh, that I had stopped his answer! But it came out
    with a run;
"Last-a week-a plenty puppy; this-a week-a puppy
    done!"
Just then my wife, my love, my life, the apple of mine
    eye,
Was seized with what seemed "mal-de-mer,"—"sick
    transit" rabbit-pie! . . .

(By James Brunton Stephens, "The Queensland Poet," from *Australian Ballads and Rhymes* . . . [London, 1888], as quoted in B. S. Donaghey in "The Chinese Restaurant Story Again: An Antipodean Version," *Lore and Language* 2 [January 1978], pp. 24–26.)

Further Ethnic Stereotype Legends

The theme of outsiders supposedly violating "our" cultural norms in outrageous ways is international, as these selected examples show.

London. *A man lived in a terrace house in a fairly poor part of town. A Pakistani family moved in several houses away. One day he heard a noise in his loft—the space between the roof and the ceiling of the top floor. When he investigated he found seventeen Pakistanis living there. They had entered the loft of one Pakistani house and spread themselves out into all the lofts along the terrace.*

Stockholm. *Many urban legends deal with the strange and sometimes criminal behavior of foreigners. Pizza shops use rat meat or pet food. Finns make a sauna out of the kitchen by turning up the oven and throwing water in it. Turks grow potatoes in the living room of their flat, and so forth. (From Dr. Svante Kjellberg, Linkoping, Sweden.)*

Istanbul. *Here in Turkey the Japanese are very much admired for their efficiency in business and their wizardly technical achievements. So we have many urban legends about them. For example, they are supposed to have developed a special kind of spectacles that show the people around you stark naked. The Japanese are also credited with developing dwarf ponies and even dwarf people—something like their dwarfed trees and shrubs in Japanese gardens. There are said to be whole armies of Japanese dwarf men and women kept hidden as a government secret. (From Fatik Ozguven, Istanbul, Turkey.)*

Saudi Arabia. *There are many Koreans working here, and recently one of them was rushed to hospital suffering from food poisoning. The doctors were concerned about the severity of the case and asked the health authority to check on the hygiene conditions where the man lived. They went to his apartment and when they opened the refrigerator they found inside a frozen human head. It turned out that a group of Koreans had had a fight and one of them had been killed. They disposed of the body by eating it a bit at a time, but they couldn't manage the head, and as it had gone bad the sick man had been poisoned. The Saudi court sentenced them to death in the usual way: their heads were chopped off in the town square. (From Richard Beal of Surrey, England, as told to him by another Englishman who lived in Saudi Arabia.)*

Australia. *I often pick up hitchhikers (the non vanishing kind) who often turn out to be Australian. When we discuss race relations in Australia they almost invariably speak confidently about an Aboriginal family who were given "a beautiful home" but burnt it all for firewood. Also various South Pacific peoples are supposed to have developed ridiculously complicated pidgin English terms for items of modern technology; for example, "Miksmasta blong Jisas" ("Mixmaster/belong/Jesus") for a helicopter. But most of these expressions do not really exist in any of the actual forms of pidgin and are only heard being used by whites to characterize natives or occasionally from natives who have picked them up from whites and then use them as a joke. (From Hugh Young of Wellington, New Zealand.)*

```
┌─────────────────────────┐
│                         │
│   K — ⓤ — PARVE         │
│   JEWISH SECRET         │
│   TAX ON FOOD           │
│                         │
└─────────────────────────┘
```

"The Jewish Secret Tax"

This label, shown actual size, was printed on pale yellow paper and found stuck on a box of generic saltine crackers at a supermarket in Hamtramck, Michigan, by Dolores Jocque.

All three elements in the top line of the label refer to the food being prepared according to Jewish dietary laws. The letter "K" means simply "Kosher." The small "u" in a circle stands for the Union of Orthodox Jewish Congregations and shows that the food underwent rabbinical supervision in its preparation. "Parve" is Yiddish for "neutral" and signifies that the contents of the package contains neither milk nor meat and thus can be combined with any other food in recipes. Many food packages include these markings, but seldom, if ever, would all three symbols appear on one package.

Whoever printed and affixed this label, however, implies that the Jewish reference of the symbols indicates that some "secret tax on food" has been paid or skimmed off, with non-Jews footing the bill. This is a claim sometimes made by anti-Semitic speakers and literature, following the reasoning that the rabbinical supervision must be costing somebody something.

A similar rumor involves the name of the now-defunct East Coast department store chain E. J. Korvettes. Some claimed that this referred to "Eight Jewish Korean Veterans."

The line of reasoning in such stories is comparable to —and just as silly as—the notion that the Procter & Gamble "moon and stars" trademark is a satanic symbol denoting that P&G is donating funds to some devil-worship cult, a story debunked in *The Choking Doberman,* chapter 6, and elsewhere. As folklorist Gary Alan Fine of the University of Minnesota has pointed out to me, "ambiguous symbols have the potential for playing off a variety of fears." He is studying similar rumors concerning the symbols of Catholicism, the Masonic orders, and other such institutions.

Another conspiracy story popular among American fundamental religious groups follows.

"The Communist Rules for Revolution"

These rules were captured in Dusseldorf, Germany, in 1919 by the Allied Forces:

1. Corrupt the young, get them away from religion. Get them interested in sex. Make them superficial. Destroy their ruggedness.

2. Get control of all means of publicity.

3. Get people's minds off their government by focusing their attention on athletics, sexy books and plays, and other trivialities.

4. Divide the people into hostile groups by constantly harping on controversial matters of no importance.

5. Destroy the people's faith in their natural leaders by holding the latter up to contempt, ridicule, and obloquy.

6. Always preach true democracy, but seize power as fast and as ruthlessly as possible.

7. By encouraging government extravagance, destroy its credit and produce fear of inflation with rising prices and general discontent.

8. Foment unnecessary strikes in vital industries, encourage civil disorders, and foster a lenient and soft attitude on the part of government toward such disorders.

9. By specious argument cause the breakdown of the old moral virtues, honesty, sobriety, continence, faith in the pledged word, ruggedness.

10. Cause the registration of all firearms on some pretext, with a view to confiscating them and leaving the population helpless.

Take time to think—seriously—of all the above.

*Then draw your own conclusions. Frightening how far
we have permitted them (the Communists)—even
helped them—to progress, isn't it?*

Copies of these "rules" show up frequently—published in religious and right-wing political periodicals,
declaimed by anti-Communist speakers, mailed to newspapers. Bob Greene, a *Chicago Tribune* columnist, had
received copies for about ten years before he finally
stopped just tossing them out and decided to look into
their authenticy. Sometime in the 1980s (unfortunately,
my clipping of his column is undated) Greene consulted
several leading authorities on Russian history and political science who assured him that the "Communist
Rules" are "a total fraud," "an obvious fabrication," "an
implausible concoction of American fears and phobias,"
and so forth.

My favorite comment, though, was Green's own: "I
always wanted to meet a Communist who was carrying
the list around, so I could ask him what 'obloquy'
means."

5

Sex and Scandal

Green M&Ms

Passion power!
Some say green M&Ms make a person irresistible

*Chaucer recommended garlic, onions and leeks.
Mushrooms, frog's bones and dried chicken tongues
also were said to do the trick.*

*Then came oysters, Spanish fly, olives, strawberries,
ginseng and Vitamin E.*

*Now, the latest substances thought to induce a
frenzy of wild passion are green M&Ms.*

*At East Texas State University, anthropology
student Denise Boesewetter recently spent weeks
interviewing people about what they thought were
aphrodisiacs. Of 46 respondents, Boeswetter reported
last month that almost half mentioned green M&Ms as
a powerful inducer of sexual desire.*

*At a University of Texas sorority house in Austin, a
large jar filled with green M&Ms is reserved for
"special occasions."*

*And at Dallas' Arts Magnet High School, the
candy's reputed powers also are a hot item on the
teen grapevine. "They make you look sexually*

*attractive," says Jana Hodges, a 17-year old senior.
"Green M&Ms are the first ones to eat when you tear
open the package."*

(Opening of a story under the byline of Stephen G.
Bloom in the *Dallas Morning News,* 22 May 1984.)

Not true, according to people who have tried them (in-
cluding me), the company that makes them, and Hal
Morgan and Kerry Tucker in their book *Rumor!* (New
York: Penguin, 1984). The book reports, however, that
T-shirts exist imprinted with "Green M&Ms Make You
Horny."

The red ones never made you horny either, so that is
not (as rumors claim) why they were removed from the
market in 1976. The reason for that action on the part
of The M&M/Mars Company was publicity concerning
the carcinogenic nature of red dye no. 2, which wasn't
the coloring agent used in this candy anyway. So PR and
not a health hazard brought on the demise of the red
ones. No actual contamination and no aphrodisiacal
power, whatever the color—just chocolate, preservative,
coloring, and folklore.

The green M&Ms rumor is not that recent, is certainly
not peculiar to Texas (as Bloom's story might suggest),
and has some variations, all features that are the hallmarks of folklore. For example, do the yellow ones make
you gay? Does giving someone a green one (or choosing
green from an offered handful) signify a homosexual
invitation? Are the brown ones bad luck, or the orange
ones good luck? Why is there no folklore about the tan
ones? (At least none that I've discovered.) And did blue
ones ever exist?

I can answer that last one, anyway. No. There were no
blue ones—ever—although some people believe that
they were once manufactured but later withdrawn as

looking too unappetizing. Several publications, quoting the manufacturer, have revealed the proportions of each color to be found in an average M&Ms package. As *Games* magazine (June 1983) put it, in a bowl of 100 you're likely to get 40 brown M&Ms, 20 yellow, 20 orange, 10 green, and 10 tan—but no sexual enhancement, except what might be provided by wishful thinking and traditional belief.

A Snake Story

A large bushy potted palm is delivered to a private home. The lady of the house signs for it, and the deliveryman departs. As she takes it into the kitchen the woman screams when she sees a snake slither out from among the leaves. Her cry brings her husband running out of the bathroom, where he has been showering. He has only a towel draped around him.

"There! There! Under the sink!" the woman screams. Her husband drops the towel as he gets down on his hands and knees for a better view under the sink. Then the family dog—excited by all the commotion—comes into the room to investigate. Seeing its naked master in this odd position, the dog curiously puts its cold nose against the man's rear end. The man starts up abruptly, banging his head on a pipe and knocking himself out cold.

His frantic wife is unable to revive him. Thinking that he may have had a heart attack or have been bitten by the snake, she calls an ambulance. As the paramedics load the unconscious nude man with the bumped head onto the stretcher, they ask her what happened, and when she explains the whole thing they laugh so hard that one man loses hold of a corner of the stretcher. Her husband is dropped to the floor and breaks his leg [arm, neck, collarbone, etc.]

This is a classic "hilarious accident" legend (see *The Vanishing Hitchhiker* for other examples). Often the sequence of mishaps begins with a man being dragged off his house roof where he has been working to adjust the

TV antenna, fix the chimney, or replace shingles. Lacking a ladder, he had tied a rope around his waist with the other end fastened to his car's bumper. A friend was supposed to drive the car slowly away, lifting him onto the roof. But his wife, unaware of his situation, drives away on an errand dragging him off the roof and along behind her.

Another typical opener for this kind of story is the exploding toilet episode discussed in the Preface. These and several other accident stories regularly end with the "laughed so hard they dropped the stretcher" motif.

Hilarious accidents involving nudity often have animals in them. In a typical variant a cat playfully takes a swing at a sensitive part of a nude man who is involved in some emergency situation; see the appendix of *The Choking Doberman* for a version of this form of the story collected from a computer bulletin board. Herb Caen told essentially the same story that I have given above involving a cat, but no snake, in a 1964 column in the *San Francisco Chronicle.* This time the woman sees a leak under the kitchen sink and calls her husband from the shower because she thinks there may be some connection between the two water lines. Caen's concluding line was, "So here we have this guy who wakes up in the hospital with a busted collarbone and the last thing he remembers is looking at a leaky pipe."

In July 1984 a Houston, Texas, radio talk show host told me a wonderful version of the snake story that started out with the delivery to a home of a living Christmas tree with its root ball wrapped in burlap. A snake emerges from the roots of the tree, and the woman of the house screams; later it reappears and she screams again. The first scream fetches her nude husband, who has the usual accident with a cat, and the second scream causes the paramedics to drop her husband's stretcher. The raconteur of this story titled it "How Was the Snake's

Christmas?" Paul Smith gives a short variant of this same one titled "A Cold Surprise" in *The Book of Nasty Legends* (London: Routledge & Kegan Paul, 1983).

"The Spider in the Yucca" in chapter 4 opens with a scene similar to many versions of this snake story—the delivery to a home of a plant infested with some dangerous creature.

♣"The Ski Accident"

BEWARE, BARE SKIER!

You know how one thing sometimes leads to another? Well, during a ski trip to New York, an Akron woman and her female friend from another city attended a wine-tasting party at the top of of a mountain. It was all downhill from there.

After a while, the Akron woman's friend received a call from Mother Nature. Since there were no restrooms atop the mountain, she decided to ski across the snow and into the trees.

She had pulled down her suit and everything was going nicely when she began slipping backward, down the mountain.

There is nothing in the downhill manual under skiing, backward, pants down. So the woman improvised. She threw out her arms in hopes of breaking the momentum of her descent.

She also broke her arm on a tree.

The ski patrol rushed the embarrassed skier to an ambulance and on to a hospital.

Outside the emergency room, waiting for her arm to be placed in a cast, the woman encountered a man whose leg had been broken.

"How did you break it?" the woman asked.

"You wouldn't believe it," he said. "I was riding a lift up the hill when I saw this woman with no pants on skiing down the hill backward. I fell right off the lift.

"By the way, how did you break your arm?"

"I, uh, I just fell down," the woman stammered.

(From a column by Steve Love in the *Akron* [Ohio] *Beacon Journal,* 14 April 1982.)

I had heard this hilarious accident legend told as a "Tourist story" about a Utah ski resort in the winter of 1979–80, and I mentioned it in the last chapter of *The Vanishing Hitchhiker* along with three other legends in which accident victims compare notes in an emergency room. Since then, "The Ski Accident" seems to have had a vigorous life in tradition and in the press.

On 6 February 1982 Ron Hudspeth of the *Atlanta Constitution* ran the story as the adventure of a young stewardess from Atlanta taking a ski vacation in Aspen, Colorado. She suffered only frostbite from slipping downhill with her bottom exposed. When she consulted her doctor back home for treatment, she saw that he had his arm in a cast. The reason? "You wouldn't believe it," laughed the doctor. "I was in Aspen skiing a few days ago and suddenly, out of nowhere came this young lady on skis with her backside exposed screaming down the mountain. . . ."

In July 1982 folklorist Ernest Baughman wrote me that he had heard the story told as true while on a visit to Indiana. The victim—a friend of a friend, skiing at an unspecified resort—had the usual accident. She asks a man wearing a cast in the ski lodge the next night what sort of accident he had suffered, and he gives the usual answer. She thought, "At least he'll never recognize me, since he was too interested in my other end to have seen my face."

By winter 1982–83 Susanna Fennema of Lawton, Oklahoma, wrote me that she had heard "The Ski Accident" told as something that had happened to a wealthy Mexican lady skiing at Vail, Colorado. Around the same time, when I was speaking by telephone on a talk show on station CKCK of Regina, Saskatchewan, a local caller

related the story as an adventure that supposedly happened to a skier from Canada vacationing at Vail. This
time a ski instructor suffers a broken leg. One year later
the December 1983 issue of *Ski* magazine reprinted it as
"A Boo-Boo to Beat Them All" from columnist Ted
Blackwell of the *Montreal Gazette:* "He assures us it's
true." In this version we're back to the falling-off-the-ski-
lift theme.

In July 1985 Cathy Brenholts of Pittsburgh, unaware
of my mention of the story in *The Vanishing Hitchhiker,*
wrote to ask about a story she had heard two years earlier
"from a friend who swears it happened to the daughter
of a friend of her mother's" at the Pennsylvania ski resort
Seven Springs on the run called North Face. The bare-
bottomed foaf streaks again!

The grand finale—so far—of the story's wanderings is
this. When I mentioned the comic skiing adventure to
folklorist Bengt af Klintberg from Stockholm he sent me
a photocopy of the same legend's appearance in January
1981 in the northern Swedish newspaper *Sundsvalls Tidning.* There, complete with a cartoon illustration, is the
story of "En kvinna i Leksands slalombackar"—a woman
at the Leksand slalom hill—who caused a Scandinavian
scandal and brought about another person's ski accident
all because she had to make a little comfort stop. (A
typical version of "The Ski Accident" was summarized in
the August–September 1985 issue of *Raka Spåret,* a magazine distributed to riders on the Swedish national rail-
ways. In the article "Moderna Myter" [Modern Myths]
ethnologist Jan Wall of the University of Göteborg is
quoted as saying that the story had spread all over Sweden in the past few years, was widely reprinted in newspapers, and appeared in a sketch on Swedish television.)

BAKVIKT

Leksand (TT)

En kvinna i Leksands slalombackar lämnade backen, åkte in i ett buskage och knäppte upp skidbyxorna för att uträtta det som uträttas måste — kissa nämligen. Men hon glömde en liten detalj. Hon hukade sig ned utan att ta av skidorna och av okänd anledning kom hon på glid.

På väg ut i backen insåg hon att något måste göras och lutade sig bakåt för att minska farten. Skarföre rådde och hon fick flera skrapsår. För att få såren omsedda uppsökte hon läkare. Ännu en skidåkare tvingades uppsöka läkaren en stund senare för en armskada. Han fick frågan hur olyckan gått till och svarade:

— Ni kommer inte att tro mig, men jag måste ändå berätta det. Jag var på väg utför slalombacken när jag fick syn på en halvnaken kvinna som kom forsande ut för backen.

— Jag tittade och tittade. Tyvärr gjorde jag det så grundligt att jag kom ur balans och körde rakt på ett träd.

Sundsvalls Tidning

"The Avon Flasher"

A woman has just finished cleaning her bathroom, including putting up a fresh roll of toilet paper, when the doorbell rings. It's the Avon lady, or rather an Avon lady, one whom she has never seen before. She invites her in and listens to her rather mediocre sales pitch.

The Avon lady asks if she may use the bathroom, and the woman says, "Yes, it's right at the top of the stairs." A few minutes later the visitor calls out to say that there is no more toilet paper, and could the woman please bring her a roll. Immediately suspicious, the woman calls the police, who tell her to stall, not to go upstairs, and to wait for them to arrive.

She calls to the visitor that she has to go to the basement to get the toilet paper and she waits nervously. Soon the police arrive and go up to the bathroom. They find a nude man waiting there.

In a variation of this story the traveling saleslady takes so long in the bathroom that the woman goes up to investigate. There she herself discovers the nude man. Both versions share with "The Hairy-Armed Hitchhiker" (chapter 6) the theme of a lone woman threatened by a man who is dressed in woman's clothing.

✈"The Green Stamps"

*This is one I have heard at least three times over
the past twenty years, each time recited as having
happened to a friend of a friend of the narrator.*

*The lady goes to her gynecologist for examination.
Before she sees him, she visits the ladies' room.
There is no paper, of course, so she resorts to
Kleenex from her purse. She also had some trading
stamps in her purse.*

*Comes exam time, and the doctor discovers that the
stamps, unbeknownst to her, of course (which would
seem terribly uncomfortable to me), have remained
with her. So he invariably makes the very
unprofessional remark, "Gosh, Mrs. So-and-So, I
didn't know they gave green stamps nowadays," or
something to that effect.*

*At least once in the telling, the lady grabbed her
clothes, fled in a huff, and never went to that doctor
again.*

(This is the version on which I based my capsule description of this story in *The Choking Doberman,* chapter 5.
It was sent to me in July 1980 by Dorothy Best of Water-
loo, New York.)

In July 1984 a woman in Gainesville, Florida, confirmed
(in my mind) that this was another urban sex legend; she
wrote that she had heard the same story told as true in
Alabama and Florida, both times by people with some
medical background. In her version the doctor did not
laugh or even mention to the patient what he had seen,
not wanting to embarrass her.

But then in October 1984 a source in Salt Lake City assured me that she had heard "The Green Stamps" told as a first-person experience by an absolutely trustworthy co-worker in 1970. She said her friend, out of necessity, had used an outdoor portable toilet at a construction site shortly before she had a gynecological examination scheduled. I was not able to verify this report, but in July 1985 I included a summary of "The Green Stamps" in a query/article I wrote for *Whole Earth Review* that was excerpted in the *San Francisco Chronicle*. The results were astounding!

First the foafs: four California women wrote to say that they had heard the story. One remembered it told in about 1965–66 in Ingram, Texas, about sixty miles from San Antonio. [Punchline: "Oh, I see you're giving Green Stamps now."] A second reader had heard the story some fifteen years ago in San Francisco attributed to a relative of the acquaintance who told it; here the doctor, nurse, and patient all had a laugh together. Third, a reader had heard it, again "some fifteen years ago" in Los Angeles, but involving Blue Chip stamps. And fourth, a Santa Rosa woman heard it attributed to a specific local gynecologist the usual fifteen years ago, but "I didn't have the nerve to ask him if it was true."

Now the zinger—from Donna DeLacy Celler of San Francisco:

I couldn't believe my eyes! MY story about the Green Stamps.

It happened like this . . . Fall 1963, Dallas, Texas. (I was Donna Young then):

I was in the middle of my third pregnancy, arrived at the OB's office, needed to go to the ladies room and did indeed substitute a tissue from my purse. A mother's purse is always full of useless and half-used items. I then proceeded into the examining room, hoisted myself on the table and into the stirrups.

The Doctor . . . sauntered in, said a few
pleasantries, and disappeared behind the sheet at the
foot of the table. Two seconds later his head appears,
his hand grasping green stamps, and he says to me.
. . . "Well, Donna, you giving these out nowadays?"

Of course, at the time I was mortified, but it didn't
prevent me from telling all my women friends
through all these years in the six cities I have lived
since that time. I never sued Dr.———nor did I
change doctors until I moved from Dallas in 1968.

In the spirit of scientific inquiry, Mrs. Celler listed for
me an account of her movements from 1963 to the present, which I assure her will be closely scrutinized by all
students of modern folklore. This may turn out to be the
first documented instance of the birth—so to speak—of
an urban legend. The Young/Celler travels-with-legend
were as follows:

1963–68	*Dallas*
1968–69	*Birmingham, Alabama*
July 1969	*To New York City*
July 1970	*Back to Birmingham*
January 1972	*To Burlington, Vermont (but says*
	she probably did not tell the story
	there)
June 1972	*Back to New York (living near*
	Croton-on-Hudson and commuting)
October 1973	*To the Bay Area (living in Marin,*
	Alameda, and San Mateo counties
	and San Francisco)

Mrs. Celler, who seems to be both the source and
carrier of this tradition, concludes, "Every time a woman
heard the story she would fall out of her chair laughing
and always told me that she told her husband and all her

friends as well." There's nothing about the dates, details, or localities of these versions to dispute Mrs. Celler's claim to primacy for this story. One thing that doesn't fit is the reported Salt Lake City recurrence of the experience, and I'm working on that one. Another anomaly—recently uncovered—is that on 19 October 1985 an absolutely credible source (wife of a prominent folklorist) told me this as a firsthand experience in the late 1950s with the ending line, "I've heard of green stamps as premiums, but this is ridiculous!" Theoretically, some direct links between the anonymous versions and the assumed original or originals could be discovered if enough further people who have heard the story come forward with more dates and places. So, write me if you've heard this!

"The Blind Date"

A young man has a blind date arranged with a
really cute girl that he hopes to make some time with.
He decides to go prepared for anything.
Earlier in the day he stops at a drugstore to
purchase condoms. Nervous and eager, he says to the
pharmacist that he is really going to score with this
chick tonight, heh, heh, heh, and all that.
When he arrives to pick up his date that evening
her father greets him at the door. It's the pharmacist
from whom he had purchased the condoms.

This story was popular in the 1940s and 1950s when
condoms were the preferred contraceptive method,
young men had endured great embarrassment to purchase them, and terms like "blind date," "make some
time," and "chick" were still current. I consider this a
rather passé urban legend, but several readers of my two
earlier books wrote to ask why I had not included it.
Perhaps the reason so many men remember it has something to do with the enduring pain of remembering all
those moments when we blurted out the wrong words at
the wrong time, maybe not exactly *this* conversation, but
other things just as humiliating.

"The Kilkenny Widow"
(An Irish Story)

Two men, John and Mick, went to Kilkenny for the day. Evening came and as they were enjoying themselves they decided they would put off the journey back to Dublin till the following day. They proposed to stay the night in the pleasant hotel they were in, which belonged to an attractive widow whom they were getting to know.

They spent an enjoyable evening in the bar and made their way to their separate rooms. However, when all was quiet, Mick made his way to the widow's room and would have been seen, if there were anyone to see him, returning to his room in the early morning. When they were leaving the widow called Mick aside. "Now I know," says she, "that you have put your names in the register, but I just want to be sure who's who," taking out a notebook and pen. Mick, a quick thinker, gave John's name and address.

Mick had forgotten all about Kilkenny until, nine months later, he had a telephone call from John, who seemed to be highly excited.

"Hello! Hello! Is that Mick? Listen, do you remember that outing we had to Kilkenny? Hello! To Kilkenny, yes. Well, I don't know what to make of it. I've had a letter from a Kilkenny solicitor. Do you remember that nice widow whose hotel we stayed in? Well, the solicitor says she has died and left me the hotel and a lot of money as well. I don't understand it."

(Text number D3, under "Legends of Revenge" in Éilís Ní Dhuibhne's article "Dublin Modern Legends: An Intermediate Type List and Examples," in *Béaloideas: The Journal of the Folklore of Ireland Society* 51 [1983], pp. 55–70, as quoted from Kevin O'Nolan, a lecturer at University College in Dublin.)

This is a popular British modern legend, mentioned in *The Choking Doberman,* page 133, and here given a specific Irish locale. A version heard in Rome appeared in Edna O'Brien's column "Hers" in the *New York Times,* 26 September 1985, p. C2.

"The Turkey Neck"
(Two Scottish Versions)

Version number A4 (collected 14 March 1982)
*It's not a story. It's true. It really is true. Well my
daughter has a friend in Bellshill, an' a fortnight ago
she was up visitin' her. An' she was tellin' her aboot
her friend. She was off her work over the New Year.
So when she came back she said to her, "Listen," she
says, "What happened?" She says, "Well, Ah broke
my wrist, but when I tell you you won't believe it."
She says, "What happened?" She says, "Well my
husband," she says, "he got that drunk," she says, "I
couldn't get him up stairs." So she left him just lyin'
on the floor. So . . . she'd a turkey for the dinner. An'
you know how the neck of a turkey it's the shape o' a
penis? You know? So the two teenage sons come in
. . . they'd been at a party. So they opened up his
ballops [trouser fly] an' they put this . . . stuck this
out. So during the night she goes, "Oh, I better go
down the stair an' see what like he is." When she
came down the stairs the cat was right in at the very
end o' it! An' she was . . . she lurched . . . she faintit
an' fell an' broke her wrist. An' that is true. That's
true.*
Version number A5 (collected 18 March 1982)
*We had been at work one night and one of my
girlfriends she said the night previous her sister had
phoned her . . . from Corby. And she said she had a
story to tell her about one of her workmates. The
lady'd come in to work . . . and she had her arm in
plaster. And she said to her, "What happened?" She*

said, "You . . . oh . . . you'll never believe it when I
tell you." She says, "Well, go on tell us and . . . try
us out anyway." So she said that her husband had had
quite a bit to drink, at New Year, and . . . he was
drunk. And she couldn't get him to bed. So she tried
to lift him but he was lying on the floor. So she
thought, "Well, I'll just leave him lying there and I'll
go to bed." So she went upstairs to bed. And the two
teenage sons had come in and found the father lying
on the floor. And . . . for a laugh . . . they went out
to the kitchenette and the turkey neck . . . was lyin'
there, and they lifted it [took it]. They'd had it for
their dinner, apparently, the turkey. And they brought
it in. So they sort of unzipped his trousers and
popped it . . . left so much of it hanging out you
know, and . . . went upstairs to bed. So during the
night the woman wokened up and she said . . . she
wondered where her husband was. And she
remembered she'd left him downstairs so she thought,
"Oh my, it'll be cold down there." So she went down
and as she opened her door into the living-room, she
put the light on, and she saw the cat . . . eating the
turkey neck and she fainted. And that was how she
broke her wrist.

(Two versions quoted from the first of three distinct
transmission chains for this story that were collected and
analyzed by Gordon McCulloch in " 'The Tale of the
Turkey Neck': A Legend Case-Study," *Perspectives on Contemporary Legend Proceedings of the Conference on Contemporary
Legend,* Sheffield, England, July 1982 [University of Sheffield: Centre for English Cultural Tradition and Language, CECTAL Conference Papers Series No. 4, 1984],
pp. 147–66.)

McCulloch, who teaches in the English and Folklife Studies Department at the University of Stirling, collected a

dozen texts of three independent versions of this story. In his paper he analyzed three topics: (1) their "flight distance" (how far the stories are said to be from their alleged source); (2) their "etiological core" (the relationship of the stories to a central meaning or idea to explain the events in them); and (3) their "lexical density" (the stories' linguistic structure compared to a popular joke cycle of the same time). It's pretty heavy stuff.

Paul Smith in his *Book of Nasty Legends* cited earlier tells "The Turkey Neck" as a prank played by two friends of the drunken man who bring him home after a night on the town. His wife is so shocked that she falls down the stairs and breaks her leg. I have heard yet another version in which the wife herself plays the prank, but she goes to sleep and forgets about him until she returns downstairs later to fetch her husband. She then faints, hits her head on the hearth, and suffers cuts and bruises. All of these variants validate McCulloch's conclusion that the primary meaning of the story is a warning that such things can happen in everyday life, while the secondary suggestion is that "It is the women who suffer."

"Caught!"
(Two variations on a theme)

1. *"The Evidence"*

A toilet kept backing up in someone's house, and no matter how hard the husband plied the plunger or how much drain opener he poured down it, the problem persisted. Finally he called a plumber to open up the line and free the obstruction for him.

The plumber soon solved the problem, but warned the guy that he shouldn't dispose of used condoms in the toilet or he'd continue to have stuck drains. But the man was amazed; he never used condoms.

He confronted his wife with the mystery, and she confessed that she had been having an affair with the milkman. So the next day the husband stayed home, ambushed the milkman, and shot him. Or rather he killed the substitute milkman who was on duty that day.

2. *"Walking the Dog"*

Then there was the husband who was in the habit of taking the family dog for a nice long walk each evening. It was good exercise for both of them, his wife felt, and the dog became so used to the routine that it positively drooled to be taken out right on schedule every night.

So when her husband was sick one evening, the wife took the dog out instead. And to her surprise the dog pulled vigorously at the leash and led her around the block to a house around the corner and began to scratch at the door. A female voice called out, "I won't be a minute, darling."

Soon the door was opened by an attractive young woman in a negligee, and the dog dashed in straight to a dish of meat that was waiting for him—as usual.

"The Bothered Bride"

*Here's the story that's making the rounds, and
everyone swears it's the gospel truth:*

*There was a big wedding in South St. Paul or Inver
Grove Heights recently, and just before the vows were
spoken, the bride turned to the assembled friends and
relatives:*

*"I want to thank you all for being here and for the
beautiful gifts you've given."*

She turned to her beaming parents:

*"I want to thank my mother and father for all
they've done for me."*

She turned to her husband-to-be:

*"And I want to thank you for sleeping with my
maid-of-honor last night!"*

*With that, on her wedding day, the bride-to-be is
said to have deposited her bouquet in either the
groom's face or over the head of her maid-of-honor
and stalked out of the church.*

*"True story, true story," chuckled East Side grocer
Matt Morelli; "I know it's true because I heard it
three times last week. Vinnie's wife heard it from a
friend who was at the wedding, someone else heard it
at the Capitol and Al Mueller told it to me Saturday
night."*

*St. Paul funeral director Al Mueller heard it from a
retired real estate salesman, and Vinnie's wife, Marie
Landis, heard it from a friend, but not someone who
was at the wedding. Rather, the friend heard it from a
friend who heard it from a friend.*

*"I don't know if it's true," said Marie, "but if it is,
that bride has a lot of guts."*

You know what that story probably is? Urban folklore . . .

(From Don Boxmeyer's column in the St. Paul, Minnesota, *Pioneer Press and Dispatch,* Midweek section, week of 7 October 1985. Bill Drew of St. Paul, who sent me the clipping, said he had heard the same story at work about two weeks before Boxmeyer wrote it up.)

"The Bothered Bride" story made a straight run across the northern tier of states and reached into Canada in late summer/early fall, 1985. Terri Taggart of Toronto wrote me in August to say that it was being told there as something that happened at a big Italian wedding, except that the groom made the speech and accused his bride of misbehavior (the "Grumbling Groom" variation). In September I heard from John Ruckes of Branford, Connecticut, that the bride had caught the groom in the bushes behind the reception hall with her maid-of-honor. Shortly after English professor Gerry O'Connor of the University of Lowell, Massachusetts, wrote to say that four students in his classes had located the story in their respective hometowns, with the bride (or groom) speaking up at a big Italian (or Irish) wedding. On 24 December 1985 the scandal sheet *World Weekly News* retold "The Bothered Bride" from a Los Angeles society columnist as something that happened in Simi Valley, California. The story ran under the banner headline "BRIDE'S WEDDING SHOCKER" and was accompanied by a photograph of a blindfolded woman wearing a bridal gown, thus providing classic read-it-in-the-newspaper pseudoverification. In every case, I suppose, it's the sort of BIG SCENE we would all love to make if we ever got a chance. Possibly, too, the story spins off from the tendency in many modern weddings for the happy couple to make grateful little speeches to their parents, attendants, and guests as part of a homemade ceremony.

6

Crime

➤"The Packet of Biscuits"

An elderly woman, traveling by bus, had a layover during her journey. She purchased a package of Oreo cookies from a vending machine in the bus terminal and located a table. She placed her cookies on the table, sat down, and proceeded to read her newspaper.

She was joined by a young man, who, to her surprise, opened the package of Oreo cookies and began to eat them. The woman, saying nothing, but giving him an icy stare, grabbed a cookie. The young man, with a funny look on his face, ate another cookie. The woman again glared and grabbed another cookie. The young man finished the third cookie and offered the last to the woman.

Completely appalled, she grabbed the cookie and the young man left. Outraged, the woman threw down her paper only to find her unopened Oreos on the table in front of her.

(Sent to me by Elizabeth Larson, a Purdue University student, after reading my account of British versions of this story in *The Choking Doberman*, pp. 191–93. "Biscuits" means "cookies" in England, and I retain the word in the title as a reminder of where this legend was first identified.)

This story of a minor crime has circulated in Great Britain since at least 1972, both in the mass media and orally. Often the man there belongs to a minority race or is an immigrant. He typically endures the situation in silence, even sometimes breaking the last cookie in half to share it, without saying a word. The woman—usually elderly, and sometimes faintly aristocratic—may also say nothing at all or may admonish the stranger, remarking something like, "We don't behave that way in this country!"

Recent versions of the legend told in Australia as well as England specify that it is a Kit-Kat candy bar which the two share, each person alternately breaking off one of the four sectioned pieces of the chocolate-covered wafer bar. Sometimes the angry woman also takes a bite out of a piece of cake the young man has on a plate in front of him before she departs. Then she discovers her own Kit-Kat in her pocket as she reaches into her purse for her ticket or keys. The young man in these versions is sometimes described as being a "punk."

Ben Miskin of Christchurch, New Zealand, sent me the following two punk versions from recent published sources:

The Sweet Taste Of Revenge?

We hear of a close encounter of the eating kind between a pensioner and punk rocker in a central city cafe. . . .

An 80-year-old lady tottered into a cafe, keen to rest her feet and reflect on the morning shopping excursion.

She orders coffee and a Moro bar [a chocolate bar] and sits down. Before long a youthful punk rocker sits at the same table opposite her.

Realising she hasn't sugared the coffee, the pensioner heads for the all important sachet on the counter.

Returning, to her horror, she discovers a portion of the Moro bar has gone. Eyeing the punk rocker she decides silence is the best defence.

Casually she picks up the Moro and eats it, from the other end, never taking her eyes off the spiked headed punk. He says nothing.

Now feeling more bold, the 80-year-old decides retribution is in order. She picks up the punk's custard square and takes a bite from it. He says nothing.

Feeling on top of the world she finishes the coffee and strolls out. Victory is hers.

Getting to the bus stop she opens her handbag for the fare. Inside: An unopened Moro bar.

(From *The Pegasus Post* of Christchurch, April 29, 1985.)

PUNK ROCKED!

She was in her seventies. After purchasing her cup of coffee and Moro bar, she gazed around the crowded coffee-bar looking for a seat. The only table available was near the door and at it sat a punk rocker with bright orange hair.

After sitting down, she realized she had left her gloves on the counter and got up. On returning, she noticed her Moro bar had been unwrapped and a bite had been taken out of it. Without saying a word, she finished her bar and coffee then calmly reached over and broke a piece off the pie the young man was about to eat. He in turn did not say a word.

Finishing the pie, she quietly got up and walked out

the door to her bus stop. She opened her purse for her bus ticket and, to her horror, saw a fully wrapped Moro bar sitting there.

(Attributed to the South Island city of Dunedin in *The New Zealand Woman's Weekly,* June 1985.)

English author Douglas Adams included the same traditional story, even incorporating the characteristic phrase "packet of biscuits," in his novel *So Long, and Thanks for All the Fish* (New York: Harmony Books, 1984). This is the fourth volume in his "Hitchhiker's Guide to the Galaxy" series. Not only does Adams's character tell the story as a true one, in the usual urban legend style (see *So Long,* pp. 106–111), but Adams himself has repeated the tale on American television talk shows, implying that it was his own personal experience.

"The Packet of Biscuits," like "Old vs. Young" in chapter 2, often deals with what is sometimes called "the generation gap." The next legend is similar in setting, characters, and action, although the theme is a bit different.

"The Guilty Dieter"

*I heard this about ten years ago at a Weight
Watchers' meeting and wondered if it was true. . . .
A dieter bought a cup of coffee and sat at a table
with a strange man, since the shop was crowded. Her
table partner ate one of two powdered sugar
doughnuts on his plate and got up to leave. When he
had left the table, the woman took a quick look
around and hastily devoured the doughnut left on the
plate. Just then the man returned with another cup of
coffee to find the woman sitting there with powdered
sugar all over her face and front.*

(Sent to me in November 1984 by Mary Martin of Los
Gatos, California, who suggested a possible connection
to "The Packet of Biscuits." This seems likely to me as
well.)

Two other California women have written me to say
that they heard the story told in connection with a reducing program, probably Weight Watchers. Tom Reilly of
Berkeley remembers hearing it about 1970 told by a New
York City co-worker as an experience of a fellow Weight
Watcher's client sipping black coffee at an automat, then
devouring a man's chocolate doughnut in one gulp.

It appears that Weight Watchers members giving their
"testimonies" have adapted a traditional legend as a
warning story, though it is possible that the event has
actually happened too. But, then, that's true of many
other urban legends as well.

"The Lottery Ticket"

I first heard this story in either 1973 or 1974, and I've heard it at least once again since.

A man is sitting in a bar with his friends. He is a recent winner of the lottery, a big prize winner as a matter of fact—in the thousands of dollars. He passes his winning ticket around the room to show it off to everyone, but when it is returned to him, it is a different ticket.

(Sent to me in January 1985 by Dennis Williams of Belleville, Michigan.)

This has the ring of a true urban legend, since the victim is not identified, the source has heard it more than once, and probably such a theft could easily be thwarted when the winning ticket was cashed in.

A counterpart to this story is mentioned in *The Choking Doberman,* chapter 6: A narcotics officer visits a high school to give an anti-drug lecture; when he passes around a joint on a plate, so that students can learn to recognize one when they see or smell it, he finds three joints on the plate when it comes back to him.

"The Shoplifter and the Frozen Chicken"

*High marks for originality of hiding-place must be
given to the lady shoplifter in Nuremberg who—
doubtless fully-laden at all other concealment
capacities—attempted to steal a frozen chicken from a
supermarket by hiding it under her hat.
Unfortunately, there was the usual blasted queue at
the cash desk, and while standing in line beneath the
burden of her refrigerated crowning glory, she finally
fainted and was taken to hospital with suspected
icing-up of the brain.*

(From Patrick Ryan, "Are You Being Robbed?" in
Punch, 16 March 1977, p. 442.)

The story of a *man* attempting to steal a frozen chicken
by concealing it in his hat appeared in Swedish newspapers in 1974. The shoplifting *lady* variant as a supposed
London occurrence showed up in English newspapers in
1976, while the 1977 version from *Punch* quoted above
makes her a German shopper. All of these variations
were supplied to me in photocopies by folklorist Bengt
af Klintberg, who told me that he encountered American
variants of the story while he was a guest lecturer at the
University of California at Berkeley.

Short news items repeating the story from Europe
have appeared in American periodicals from time to
time, I've been told, and a correspondent from London
wrote me in 1981 that she had just heard a radio report
about a woman fainting in a supermarket because she
had a frozen chicken hidden in her hat. Possibly such
media reports have given rise to the occasional appear-

ances of the story as an urban legend. The basic situation, of course, is similar to the old "Spider in the Hairdo" legend, in which a woman who has fainted is discovered to have some unexpected thing concealed in her hair (see *The Vanishing Hitchhiker,* chapter 4).

In his autobiography, *Tiger of the Snows,* Tenzing Norgay, Sir Edmund Hillary's companion in climbing Mount Everest, relates "a story told among the Sherpas" that may be related to this legend. Two lamas come to a house where a woman is cooking sausages, and one tries to steal some when she leaves the room by hiding them under his pointed hat. When the woman suddenly returns, the other lama changes the prayer chant to say "the sausages are showing," which he repeats over and over again, trying to warn his companion to conceal them better. But the other lama can only reply as he hops about in pain, "I don't care if the whole pig is showing. My head is burning up!"* I am grateful to Leslie Fish of El Cerrito, California, for calling this reference to my attention.

In Autumn 1985 the shoplifting story going around was about a pregnant woman supposedly arrested on her way out of a sporting goods store on suspicion of stealing a basketball. "Too neat. Sounds like a fable," commented Herb Caen of the *San Francisco Chronicle* (12 September 1985). I second the motion.

---

*See *Tiger* (New York: Putnam's, 1955), pp. 98–99.

A Drug-Smuggling Legend

MIAMI—*A federal undercover agent talks about the case of the baby who did not move. An attendant on a flight from Colombia to Miami became suspicious and called U.S. Customs agents to have a look. They discovered that the baby had been dead for some time. Its body had been cut open, stuffed with cocaine and sewn shut.*

In Miami, federal agents are no longer surprised by such gruesome discoveries. This is a city that almost thrives on crime. . . .

(From a story in the *Washington Post* on Miami's crime problems by Mary Thornton, 25 March 1985.)

CORRECTIONS: *In the opening paragraph of an article last Monday on crime in Miami, The Washington Post recounted a story that cannot be substantiated. The story, told to a Post reporter several years ago by a Miami undercover agent, involves the smuggling of cocaine into the United States in the body of a dead baby.*

Clifton Stallings, a spokesman for the U.S. Customs Service in Miami, said "the story has been in circulation for some time. No one at Customs in Miami can verify it."

Vann Capps, a Customs official in Miami, said he heard the story in a 1973 training course for inspectors at Hofstra University. "They gave us different concealment techniques from past seizures, and this one involved cocaine concealed in the dead baby's body," Capps said. He said he believes the incident was alleged to have occurred at either the

*Miami airport or John F. Kennedy International
Airport in New York.*

*But Customs spokesman Jim Mahan said yesterday
that, while the story is widely known, he could find no
one at headquarters here who could confirm it.*

(*The Washington Post,* 30 March 1985.)

This example, a typical one, illustrates how law enforce-
ment personnel and journalists—though both concerned with evaluating the truth of reported events—
may be as susceptible as the rest of us to believing a
bizarre or thrilling story just because it seems plausible.
In the 15 April 1985 *New Republic* (p. 7), the lead article
on "The Dope Dilemma" alluded to the *Washington Post*'s
original report as an example of how vicious the drug
trade has become. Their story, to my knowledge, was
never retracted.

There are other apocryphal horror stories about drug
use and drug smuggling, including a widespread account
told during the 1960s of LSD users staring directly at the
sun until they became blind. An urban legend about LSD
being sold to children in the form of cartoon-character
lick-and-stick transfers is discussed in *The Choking Doberman,* chapter 6.

"The Helpful Mafia Neighbor"

A couple in a wealthy suburb of Chicago [New York, Los Angeles, Philadelphia, etc.] have some quiet, unassuming neighbors who are rumored to have Mafia ties. One weekend when the couple has been away their home is broken into, and upon their return they discover that several expensive appliances, art pieces, furs, jewelry, and so forth are missing.

They ask their nice neighbors if they had observed any suspicious activity during their absence, explaining what has happened. The neighbors had failed to notice the burglary, but the soft-spoken husband advises the couple not to report the crime right away, just go to bed and let him make a few phone calls.

The next morning all of their missing property is on the front porch.

A variation of this story has the Mafia acquaintances who live in a different suburb invite them to a dinner party. When the couple is ready to drive back home, they discover that their car has been stolen. Their host tells them not to worry but to come in for another drink while he makes a phone call. An hour later their car is at the curb. In a related tradition, the client or patient with Mafia ties offers his lawyer (doctor, etc.) a hit job in lieu of a fee. The offer is declined, or may jokingly be changed to just breaking someone's legs; and then the professional man is horrified when the crime is promptly carried out.

✄"The Attempted Abduction"

Store abduction rumors flying,
but police say they're not true

It sounds like a real juicy news story.

A woman was shopping with her child at a Beloit [Wisconsin] department store when she turned her back for a moment. The next thing she knew, her child was gone. Store officials blocked off exits and searched the store.

The child was found in the bathroom with two women who had cut her hair and put different clothes on her. The two women supposedly were released so the store could avoid "bad publicity."

There's just one catch. Not a word of the story is true, according to the Beloit Police Department, which investigated the persistent rumor.

"We've come up with absolutely nothing," said Chief John Mizerka, who said officers tracked down various leads to determine if the incident ever occurred.

The rumor began surfacing several weeks ago, died down somewhat and has since resurfaced. No one seems to know its source, but it seems that Beloit is not the only city where it is circulating.

The rumor obviously had picked up steam by this week when two Milwaukee television stations called Beloit after receiving anonymous tips about a child abduction that supposedly occurred at a department store here.

The rumors have come to the Daily News *in the*

form: "I heard it from a friend who heard it from a
friend who knows a clerk at the store."

One Beloiter who heard about it was Arnold
Johnson.

"My first impression was it just didn't make sense,"
he said. "There are too many flaws in the story."

The store mentioned in the rumor is Shopko. Store
officials said they are well aware of the rumors and
would like them to stop.

"I assure you, there's no truth to it happening in
any one of our stores," said Gene Bankers, vice
president of Shopko, which is based in Green Bay. "If
we did (have any knowledge of it), we would be
alerting the police and newspapers, I can assure you."

Bankers added that Shopko officials are trying to
"track down the source of the rumor."

He noted that similar rumors have been reported
throughout the state, and not just at Shopko stores.
In Green Bay, the rumor concerns an abduction at a
mall. But despite all the rumors no one with direct
knowledge of such an abduction ever has come
forward, Bankers said.

The Beloit rumor was described to Green Bay
Press-Gazette columnist Donald Langenkamp, who has
done a series of columns on abduction rumors.

"That's basically it, word for word," said
Langenkamp.

He said the rumor there has been occurring for
about the past two years, but has picked up
momentum in recent weeks, and that similar stories
have been reported throughout the Fox River Valley.
Langenkamp has tried unsuccessfully to track down
the source of the rumors.

Not coincidentally, the LaCrosse Tribune in the
past week received a letter to the editor about child

abductions, said Grant Blum, a reporter there. The letter's author gave 17 tips about keeping children safe from abduction.

At the end of the letter, the woman explained that it was serious business because in nearby Dubuque, Iowa, an abduction had occurred at a mall. The woman then described an abduction that was almost identical to the one rumored in Beloit.

Blum said a reporter at the paper checked on the Dubuque story and found it to be false.

(Story by *Beloit Daily News* writer Roger Schneider published 1 December 1983.)

I quote in full this detailed account of a reporter's fruitless attempt to verify "The Attempted Abduction" because it is so typical of numerous appearances of the story in the past few years. Most versions describe the locked doors of the store, the missing child found in a bathroom, the cut hair (often dyed as well), the switch of clothing, and the supposed suppression of the incident by the store, the police, or the media. And once the press gets hold of the story, its appearance in earlier years or in surrounding communities becomes known. Invariably the managers of specific stores named in the legend declare that it is completely false, and occasionally someone eventually points out the story's obvious flaws. (As one attorney in St. Louis who was asked about the story remarked to a reporter, "How could you dye a kid's hair in a public restroom? I'd rather give a cat a bath.")

But, sooner or later, usually sooner, the same plot pops up again and again in a community, often in the context of a warning to keep track of one's small children while shopping. It is this sound advice combined with recent publicity surrounding real-life cases of child abduction that helps to keep the old legend alive.

In *The Choking Doberman* I suggest the possible deriva-
tion of "The Attempted Abduction," a lucky escape
story, from a much older legend about a crime against a
child that is actually carried out, called "The Mutilated
Boy." A gruesome tale of sexual mutilation and murder
inspired by racial or religious prejudice, the mutilation
legend can be traced to such early forms as Chaucer's
"Prioress's Tale" and related anti-Semitic medieval folk
ballads, then up to contemporary accounts of a little
white boy supposedly castrated by a gang of blacks or
another minority in a public restroom. The two legends
overlap in that they are often set in shopping malls or
department stores, but they differ because the little girl
is always rescued with no harm done other than having
her appearance altered or at worst being sedated with a
drug or chloroform by the would-be abductors.

I also wrote in *The Choking Doberman* that one or the
other of these two restroom legends seems to peak in the
United States in about a five-year cycle, with the latest
surge in 1980. But my book had not yet been published
before "The Attempted Abduction" began a new round
of popularity, as the above 1983 example shows for the
Midwest. Also, late that year I started getting calls and
letters about the story from the Eastern states, then from
the Midwest, and then (very strongly) from Texas and
the West coast. On 14 December 1983 the *Staten Island
Advance* ran a story on the spread of the legend in New
York and in Baltimore. Around Christmastime in Salt
Lake City the same rumor was rampant that a young girl
had narrowly escaped kidnapping during a shopping trip
in the usual traditional circumstances.

All through spring and summer 1984 news stories
about local appearances of the story came out in Houston and several other Texas cities; St. Louis; Richmond,
Virginia; New Orleans; and elsewhere. Inquiries from
coast to coast reached me; and with predictable consist-

CAPTAIN EASY   BY CROOKS & LAWRENCE

© 1983 Newspaper Enterprise Association, Inc.

The study of urban legends inspires a comic strip.

ency they all told very much the same story as heard locally from similar second- and third-hand oral sources.

The "Action Line" columns of local newspapers that deal directly with readers' questions are often forced to check repeatedly the possible validity of attempted-abduction rumors. For example, in the "Ask Adam" feature in the *Amarillo Globe-Times* (4 May 1984), after ascertaining the total fictionality of the story, the columnist remarked, "Some graduate student in sociology should do a study of these rumors. . . . " Columnist Gaye Le-Baron of the *Press Democrat* of Santa Rosa, California, wrote to her readers on the same day in May, "Calm yourselves. It's just this year's story." And "Action Line" author Judy Bargainer of the *Abilene Reporter-News* had to contend with a correspondent who insisted, "I have heard this story from three different people who have no contact with each other, so I'm pretty sure it isn't just the figment of someone's imagination." Bargainer's reply was, "The reason you didn't read about the little girl in the *Reporter-News* is, we didn't know about it. . . . we would all like to know about it, starting with the Police Department."

My own correspondents have supplied various bits of

information on how the story has been circulated and
varied. For example, one wrote me that he had found
"The Attempted Abduction" printed up on a poster and
taped to the wall of a booth in a flea market in San
Antonio in Summer 1984. A New Jersey woman reported
that she heard the legend from the president of her local
PTA, who in turn had heard it reported at a convention.
A couple from North Carolina wrote me that when they
returned home from six weeks abroad a close friend
caught them up on all the news, including this legend
attached to a nearby shopping mall. But another friend
later told them that she had heard a mother in a day-care
center say it had happened in a downtown department
store, while a third friend believed it had actually occurred in a store in Mansfield, Ohio, where she had
previously lived.

One of the best concise reports of two variations of the
legend came to me from Lee Armitage, 13, of Fairfax,
Virginia:

> *My mom's friend told her about a little boy around
> 7 years old. It seems that the boy and his mother
> were shopping in the "Toys R Us" store and the boy
> wandered a little bit away from his mother to go look
> at something. A few minutes later, this mother started
> looking for the boy. She couldn't find him. Crying,
> she rushed up and told a clerk, who immediately
> locked the doors. Everyone searched. They found the
> boy, with two men. Only his hair was cut and his shirt
> was changed so he would look different.*
>
> *When my family went to the beach, in Sea Island,
> Georgia, my aunt, who lives in Alabama, heard the*
> exact same story *only it was a girl!*

Ann Landers had her share of embarrassment with
"The Attempted Abduction" starting with her 21 November 1984 column in which she quoted a standard

version that had been sent to her as an account of something that had happened "last week," as heard by a reader who signed herself "West Coast Warning." Tom Forstrom of the Salem, Oregon, *Statesman Journal,* who had interviewed me the July previous, caught the legend in Ann Landers's column even before it ran in his paper, and he wrote an advance story warning readers that the shocking anecdote was untrue. He described the dismayed reaction he got from one of Landers's secretaries when he tried to telephone the columnist in Chicago. Ann herself was on a speaking tour, and her column that day ran in the form in which it had already been circulated to papers all over the country.

In her 7 January 1985 column, Ann Landers reminded her readers of the story and named the Salem, Oregon, paper and two others from Iowa and Niagara Falls, all of which had writers who spotted the legend for what it was. "The face with the egg on it is mine, folks," she commented. At least one reader was not satisfied with this correction (or perhaps had missed her apology); on Valentine's Day 1985, Ann Landers ran yet another letter identifying this and other popular recent stories as legends. Signed "BS Detector in Chicago," this letter concluded, "Reminding people to watch their kids is one thing. Scaring the pants off them is another." But by now Ann Landers was getting a bit testy; she snapped back in reply, "I bit. So what? It was an honest mistake." The second letter she printed that day described an actual lost child incident and gave a list of tips for parents shopping with tots. In effect, the message carried in a piece of folklore was balanced with a straightforward literal statement of the same advice. Also, once again, a popular advice column was both a purveyor of modern folklore and a vehicle for publicizing the folkloric nature of a current story.

In any case, "The Attempted Abduction" was still alive

in the Midwest more than a year after the Beloit, Wisconsin, example quoted above. On 18 March 1985 columnist David Fryxell of the *Telegraph Herald* of Dubuque, Iowa, started a story, "Did you hear the one about the little girl abducted at Target when her mother's back was turned? Or maybe it was at Kennedy Mall, or K mart." And after a nice account of the spread and acceptance of the story by various writers, Fryxell commented, "Reporters and Ann Landers could have saved some trouble by asking Jan Harold Brunvand first." But, if there's one lesson I've learned from my research in urban legends, it is that they have a life of their own which is completely separate from attempts to suppress or expose them as fictional. I could run ads with the Super Bowl broadcast saying that the latest hot legends are pure folklore, and still some people would never get the message or would pass on the story itself rather than the exposé.

Coming back to another point touched on in the text quoted above, legends like "The Attempted Abduction" do have a positive function in warning people about *typical* hazards and alerting them to be careful. For example, a news story in the *Chicago Tribune* on New Year's Day 1985 described how milk cartons produced for a local dairy would soon be carrying pictures of missing children in hopes that they might be identified and reported to authorities. Cmdr. Joe Mayo of the Youth Division of the Chicago Police Department was quoted:

Mayo said that recently a child and her mother were shopping in a large Chicago area department store when the woman looked up to find that her daughter was gone. Security guards cordoned off the building exits and found the young girl alone in a rest room.

"They cut her long hair and dyed it brown," Mayo said. "Whoever it was changed her clothes. It happens that quickly."

Other writers and speakers have made the same assumption that the abduction-attempt story they have been told was an authentic case, and I have even heard of the legend being told during a congressional hearing on urban crime. Very likely the widespread legend with its spurious details has gained some credibility from several widely publicized actual cases of missing children, in particular the Adam Walsh case, which was the subject of an ABC television movie first broadcast in October 1983 and subsequently rerun. Walsh disappeared in Florida from a toy department while shopping with his parents.

𝒴"The Hairy-Armed Hitchhiker"

To: ALL STAFF   *Date: November 17, 1983*

From: Deputy Robert Wohler
BERRIEN COUNTY SHERIFF'S DEPARTMENT

Subject: Tips to Make Your Holidays Happy Days
  *Case #74685-83. Mary Smith had been shopping at
the local Jolly Green Giant Supermarket. The time
was approximately 7:30 P.M. and the parking lot was
lighted only by the overhead lights. Mary had just
finished her shopping and was taking her packages to
her car. When she arrived at her car she found a
woman sitting in her car. The woman gave Mary a sad
story and asked for a ride. Mary then placed her
packages in the back seat and told the woman she
would be right back as she had other packages in the
store. Mary then went to the store and got Security.
Security accompanied Mary to her car where the
woman was removed from the vehicle and found to
be a man. What could have been the results? Fiction?
No, fact! It did happen. Only the names used are
fictional.*

(From a memorandum distributed in the State of
Michigan Department of Social Services. The case description is followed by seven numbered paragraphs of
good advice for avoiding crime and accidents.)

Fact? No, fiction! This has been a popular American
urban legend since early 1983, and it is based on a story
known much earlier in England. Lately I have found

older American counterparts for the traditional English prototype as well. The title used above refers to the many versions in which the driver herself recognizes that the passenger is a man in woman's clothing by spotting his hairy and muscular arms (or legs) extending out from the shirt (or pants) cuffs. Another title might be "The Hatchet in the Handbag," since the disguised man sometimes escapes but leaves a purse or shopping bag behind that is discovered to contain a hatchet. Alternatively the man is sitting on the hatchet, and he may be recognized by his men's shoes or by his wig falling off when the security officer arrives and removes him from the car.

English versions of the story tend to have the woman driver rescue herself rather than relying on outside aid. Having seen through the disguise, she asks her passenger to get out of the car on the pretense of needing to check her tail lights or the inflation of a tire. Once free of the suspicious passenger, she speeds away, only to discover the concealed hatchet later.

In a news report from 1834 pointed out by an English folklorist, a man dressed as a woman leaves behind a reticule (handbag) on a coach, and it is found to contain "a brace of" (two) loaded pistols. It is probably this old story that was revived as "The Hairy-Armed Hitchhiker" during the English "Yorkshire Ripper" scare of 1977.

Richard M. Dorson's book *Negro Folktales in Michigan* (Cambridge, Massachusetts: Harvard University Press, 1956) contains a story said to have taken place shortly after the Civil War about an attempted robbery in a horse and buggy that has almost identical details. The young driver spots the stubble of a beard under his passenger's bonnet, so he contrives to lose his own hat and then asks the old woman to recover it for him while he reins back the skittish horses. Then he races away from her. The conclusion: "He picks up the basket and looks in it, to give it to his wife, and there's two Colt 44's in there, and eight hundred dollars in cash money." As Dorson comments in his note, "Here is a fine example of the allegedly true happening that conceals a migratory legend."

Another American version of what seems to be the same English legend collected in rural Kentucky by Leonard W. Roberts was published in his book *South from Hell-fer-Sartin* (Lexington: University of Kentucky Press, 1955), p. 200. Here a man riding horseback along a lonesome mountain ridge offers a ride to a woman dressed in black whom he sees crying by the side of the road and holding onto a satchel. What follows in the story contains several close analogues to details of the modern legend:

When he got her up behind him he seed a big dirk knife slip out her shirt sleeve, you know, and that scared him. Well, he run under a limb a-purpose, knocked his hat off, and told her to jump down and get his hat. And when she jumped down to get it, he put the spurs to the hoss and away he went out of the pine country. She commenced to hollerin', "Throw off the budget, throw off the satchel, throw off the satchel."

When the man gets to a town he tells people there what happened, and he is told that a man dressed as a woman has been robbing people. They look into the satchel and find it to be full of money.

7

Products, Professions, and Personalities

♣"The Economical Car"

The following story recently made the rounds in Detroit and has probably swept the country. It has not been verified but is good enough to bear repetition for the benefit of those in the trade who, as yet, may not have heard it.

A customer in Philadelphia took delivery on a 1948 Chevrolet. He filled the car with gas and started over the Pennsylvania Turnpike for Pittsburgh. At the half-way mark on the Dream Highway he pulled into the Howard Johnson Restaurant and Service Station for a bite to eat and a check-up on the new car. He was surprised to find out that he had used very little gasoline. Back on the highway he headed for Pittsburgh with an eye on the fuel indicator. At the end of the trip, which is about 300 miles, the car had consumed 4 gallons of gasoline. On the return trip the same thing happened: 300 miles on 4 gallons of gas.

In the meantime Chevrolet engineers were frantically trying to locate an experimental model which had been tagged in error for delivery to a dealer. When the astonishing mileage report was

*relayed to the factory by the Philadelphia dealer,
arrangements were made for the return of the
experimental model to a greatly relieved group of
Chevrolet engineers.*

(From T. A. Jenkins's column "Detroit Reporter" in
Automotive Digest, September 1948, p. 74. Harry Cannon
of Myakka City, Florida, sent me a copy of this item.)

This is a recurrent apochryphal story. Here it occurs in
the postwar period, when new cars were predicted to
share the technological advances developed in wartime.
A reader's letter in *Car Life* (February 1963) asked about
a 1962 Plymouth with a special carburetor designed to
get 48 to 56 miles per gallon. The editor remarked that
variations of that story had been "popping up for the last
50 years or so." Later the story was told as a form of
wishful thinking, when oil shortages caused gasoline
prices to zoom. Catherine Harris Ainsworth of Niagara
County (New York) Community College collected a text
of "The Economical Car," again a Chevrolet, from a
student, in December 1973, during the height of the
Mideast oil crisis: see "Gasoline Folklore," *New York Folklore* 2 (1976), pp. 111–13. In *The Vanishing Hitchhiker* I
quote a 1978 incident of an Associated Press reporter
trying to trace the source of the same story attached to
an experimental Ford that was said to get 1,000 miles per
tank of fuel.

Often it is claimed that the oil companies were cooper-
ating with automobile manufacturers to suppress the
wonder car (or just its special carburetor); usually the car
buyer is said to have been given a large cash payoff
($10,000 in the New York version, $30,000 in the AP
story) by the company, as well as a new car, in return for
keeping quiet.

In the June 1980 issue of *Popular Science* (p. 67), the

editor debunked several miracle car stories under the headline "Running on Hot Air." He wrote that without exception all the old stories about cars running on water, on compressed air, on the power stored in permanent magnets, or with a special carburetor that doubles or triples normal mileage can never come true until some-one finds "new laws of physics that replace or supersede those we use now."

The *Wall Street Journal* led off a front-page story on 29 March 1982 with "The Magic Carburetor" story. The headline for this piece was "Myths of Motown: Detroit Demons Help Create Series of New Legends."

Product Misuse Legends and Legal Horror Stories

✺ *"The Lawnmower Accident"*

Horror stories about unfair judgments circulated among insurers can drive rates up, even if these stories are unrepresentative or false. The [company name] advertising campaign told of a judgment against a lawnmower manufacturer for injuries suffered when the plaintiff lifted the lawnmower to cut hedges. No one can verify that this case actually occurred. Nevertheless, it is often repeated and doubtless confirms the impression of ratesetters that insurance rates must anticipate the wildest judgments. In this atmosphere, the perception of reality is more important than reality itself.

(From Anita Johnson, "Behind the Hype on Product Liability," *Forum* 14 [1978], p. 324, as quoted in *The Choking Doberman* and discussed there along with the variant in which two men lift the mower together and each cuts off eight finger tips.)

✺ *"The Butane Lighter"*

It came to me on official-looking US Dept. of Transportation stationery, but it's a hoax. I mean the story that two Union Pacific welders were killed when a spark ignited their butane lighters, which exploded "with the force of three dynamite sticks." Sighs UP Flack Al Krieg: "That story swept the country the past

month but we have no record of such an accident. It
keeps popping up everywhere. Some myths die hard."

(From Herb Caen's column in *The San Francisco Chronicle*, 21 December 1979, partially quoted in *The Choking Doberman* with reference to variants, including one in which actor/comedian Richard Pryor's burn accident was supposed to have been caused by a butane lighter.)

⊱*"The Contact Lenses"*

Reports that radiation from electric arcs or sparks can cause contact lenses to fuse to the eye are false, says the American Academy of Ophthalmology. The phony bulletins, which have been widely distributed, apparently are based on distortions of two cases, said Dr. Bruce E. Spivey, AAO's executive vice president. In one case a welder reportedly was blinded by an electrical flash, but an investigation showed his injury was not caused by the flash and that his eyesight returned to normal in a few days. The other report that an electric arc caused contact lenses to fuse to the cornea is medically impossible, Spivey said.

(A follow-up story in the *Chicago Tribune*, in June 1983, after reporting several weeks of rumors circulating orally and via printed fliers that the cornea/contact lens fusing had occurred somewhere in the East or Midwest.)

This story is discussed with further examples and variants in *The Choking Doberman*. At least one insurance company issued a loss prevention memo to counter the rumors. The absurdity of the story is suggested by a comment quoted from a University of Maryland Hospital physician in the *Baltimore Sun* (17 March 1983). Dr. Barry

M. Weiner said, "It is a physical impossibility to dry up the fluid in your eyes. You'd have to stick your head in a blast furnace to do that. . . . [And removing the cornea] would be like pulling off your ear."

Similar to these three above samples of product misuse legends are "The Microwaved Pet or Baby" and stories mentioned in *The Choking Doberman* about bizarre superglue accidents, supposedly exploding "Atomic Golfballs," allegedly addictive additives in Marlboro Lights, and the rumored horrible-death-by-shrinking Levi's. A step removed, but still pertinent to this theme, are the many food-contamination rumors and legends as well as the unverifiable stories about illegal drugs, such as "Mickey Mouse Acid." Modern folklore even infiltrates the legal profession, as shown by the following two examples.

Legal Horror Stories

*"Atrocity stories" [refers to] citation of cases that
seem grotesque, petty or extravagant: a half-million
dollar suit is filed by a woman against community
officials because they forbid her to breast-feed her
child at the community pool; a child sues his parents
for "mal-parenting"; a disappointed suitor brings suit
for being stood up on a date; rejected mistresses sue
their former paramours; sports fans sue officials and
management; and Indians claim vast tracts of land . . .*

(Listed, with supporting citations, in a discussion of
the supposed "litigation explosion" by Marc Galanter in
his article "Reading the Landscape of Disputes: What
We Know and Don't Know (and Think We Know) About
Our Allegedly Contentious and Litigious Society," in
UCLA Law Review 31 [1983], pp. 10–11.)

*Martha Fineman presents a compelling account of
the impact of reformers' "horror stories" on the
shaping of divorce reform in Wisconsin:*
*[This kind of story] symbolized and defined for the
reformers the reform that was needed. These horror
stories had as central characters a deserving but
victimized wife, a villainous and selfish husband, and a
legal system which closed not only the eyes, but the
ears of justice in the name of property rights to leave
the wife and children destitute and abandoned. . . .*
*Many of the horror stories were unsubstantiated,
came from only one source, occurred decades earlier,
or were the results of decisions by judges in different
states, but the reformers adopted them uncritically*

*and incorporated them as the central images in the
rhetoric of their reform. . . .*

*The stereotypical housewife horror story
encouraged the reformers to argue that legal
institutions were systematically biased against women
in resolving the economic incidents of divorce. This
may have been accurate in terms of the cases the
feminists compiled to support their arguments. There
is a question whether it was accurate from an
historical perspective.*

*And, it is even less clear, however, that it was
accurate in terms of all, or even most, contemporary
divorce cases in Wisconsin.*

(Quoted by Galanter in the same article from which
the preceding example comes [footnote 279, pages 64–
65], and quoted in turn there from Fineman's 1983 article in *Wisconsin Law Review.*)

Professor Galanter of the University of Wisconsin–
Madison Law School kindly supplied a copy of his article,
in which he suggests that legal "horror" or "atrocity"
stories are a form of elite folklore comparable to urban
legends and known mostly among lawyers. His conclusion on the amount of litigation (p. 64) "is not to deny
that there have been increases, even dramatic ones, in
litigation rates or in the occurrence of lawsuits unlike
those brought earlier . . . [but] that elite ways of inter-
preting these phenomena are also part of the story."

Redemption Rumors

WINSTON-SALEM, N.C.—*Somewhere today hundreds of people are piling up mountains of empty cigarette packs in garages and basements.*

They are saving them for some little boy or girl who needs time on a kidney dialysis machine, or for someone's in-law who knows of a tobacco company that will redeem the packs for other medical equipment.

These collections have been going on for years. The unfortunate fact about these charitable acts is that there is no basis for the often heard rumors.

R. J. Reynolds Tobacco Co. recorded 77 such inquiries from residents in 28 states in 10 months one year.

(From a press release dated 29 March 1985 distributed by the R. J. Reynolds Tobacco Company and sent to me by Seth Slabaugh of *The Muncie* [Indiana] *Star.*)

Folklorist Gary Alan Fine picked up the term "redemption rumors" from a Tobacco Institute spokesman who referred to these recurrent and totally fictional traditions about saving a large quantity of useless things with the belief that one can redeem them with the manufacturer to provide a major medical benefit for a needy patient. People's helpful instincts in such efforts are commendable, even if their information about such exchange programs is based on hearsay. Yet they work year after year to save thousands of empty cigarette packages (or the red cellophane opener strips), or pull tabs from aluminum cans, or the tags attached to tea bags, believing that they are in this way earning such necessities for a poor, blind, or sick child as a seeing-eye dog, a wheelchair, an iron lung, or time on a kidney dialysis machine.

In a paper delivered at the American Folklore Society annual meeting in 1984 Professor Fine adapted the term "redemption rumors" to another meaning: he believes that in a sense people who so earnestly save these useless objects are also trying to redeem *themselves* for their bad habits of using products containing tobacco, alcohol, or caffeine. Even when the items saved are soda-can pull tabs there may be the guilt factor because of drinking sugared beverages of little food value. Saving the package parts for a good cause compensates, at least psychologically, Fine suggests, for the poor nutrition.

Thus it seems that everybody can feel good about these efforts—except perhaps the companies who are embarrassed by having to debunk all these well-meaning but misguided collecting efforts. And nobody is hurt by them—except perhaps the individuals who are themselves embarrassed for being taken in by a very old rumor. So it amounts to a little embarrassment in exchange for a good dose of self-satisfaction. As for the needy young patients, they are not suffering, since no such children awaiting the collection of a million cigarette packs really exist—except in folklore. In fact, most kidney dialysis costs nowadays are completely covered by government programs and insurance payments.

The earliest specific reference to the redemption rumors that Fine located comes from 1957, although one undocumented source mentions them existing as early as 1936. Certainly there have been genuine redemption campaigns, involving specific parts of packages sent in for prizes, sponsored by American manufacturers since around the turn of the century. And in 1969 to 1970 General Mills did actually provide kidney dialysis machines for hospitals through a carefully monitored coupon redemption program. But the apochryphal redemption claims for cigarette packages, pull tabs, and the like are anonymous, unrelated to any genuine proof-of-purchase exchange program, variable as to how many items must be saved and what the medical benefit is, and keyed to an emotional description of "little Johnny" lying destitute in the hospital. In short, these stories are typical urban folklore.

Tobacco companies are most commonly said to be the participants in these redemption schemes, and over the years the company and industry spokespersons have issued dozens of press releases like the one quoted above and have replied to hundreds of inquiries from individuals and the press. Other denials are regularly carried in the "Action Line" sections of newspapers or in the advice columns (i.e., Ann Landers on 22 November 1982).

It appears that even these factual explanations have acquired folkloristic touches. For example, the term "cruel hoax" appears frequently in news releases and stories based on them, but there is no evidence that anyone has ever deliberately planted such rumors either to increase sales or to embarrass companies. A persistent statistic in the stories is the one about seventy-seven inquiries from twenty-eight states in ten months. Professor Fine was given the same figures applied to the Tobacco Institute itself for the period "January through October 1968," while an article in *Parade* (17 October 1971) quoted these figures as applying simply to an unspecified ten-month period and only to the R. J. Reynolds Company. Evidently someone in the industry once counted the inquiries up to seventy-seven, and the PR people have been quoting and requoting this number ever since. Lately there may be some confusion in people's minds between Reynolds Tobacco and Reynolds Aluminum, since the recycling centers operated by the latter have become the particular targets for people who have collected pull tabs. This version of the rumor is called "a cruel hoax" (as usual) in a United Press International story published in the *Salt Lake Tribune* on 15 February 1985.

Professor Fine has collected 137 newspaper accounts of redemption rumors. Invariably these are debunking stories, usually written after earnest local people or civic groups have amassed gigantic accumulations of useless items and are searching for a place to turn them in. Cigarette packages are completely worthless, but at least the pull tabs can be recycled; of course, it would be more efficient to save the cans themselves. No matter how often or how emphatically the rumors are denied, they show no signs of disappearing.

Following is a recent example of a news story that sums up very well just how quickly the stories spread, how trusting the collectors are, and how diligently the reporters must be to once again look into the whole matter:

PULL TAB COLLECTION FOR KIDNEY PATIENT IS JUST A HOAX
BY GREG MAYNARD

If you are collecting tabs from beer and pop cans for a kidney patient in Indianapolis, you can stop. The whole thing is a hoax.

Several local Brownie troops and parents, grandparents and friends of the troop members have been collecting tabs for the past several months in an effort to give a little boy in Indianapolis free time on a kidney dialysis machine.

Juanita Callahan, a grandmother of a local Brownie and mother of a Brownie troop leader, told The Star the local rumor was that a little boy in an Indianapolis hospital would get 2 free minutes on a dialysis machine for every tab collected.

That same story, in a slightly different form, has been reported in several different states.

Recently, the hoax appeared in Jackson, Minn., where a 10-year-old girl would get 1 free minute on a dialysis machine for every 100 tabs collected.

Several charitable groups in Jackson collected 19 gallon pails of the tabs and attempted to turn them in. At that point a snag developed: Nobody knew anything about the little girl.

In the Muncie hoax, basically the same thing happened. Mrs. Callahan said that after collecting tabs for a while she thought it would be a good idea to send the little boy a card to cheer him up, but nobody knew anything about the boy.

"I asked my daughter to find out where the little boy was, and she asked a friend who told the troop leaders about it. My daughter's friend just kept hem-hawing around and never told her anything," Mrs. Callahan said.

"It all started out when the girls [in the Brownie troop] innocently thought that this would be a good way to earn a service badge for themselves and the troop. Eventually, parents and grandparents were collecting them, and I had some people I work with at Dayton-Walther collecting them."

Mrs. Callahan said after she got no definite answer about the boy's whereabouts, she called Ball Hospital and three hospitals in Indianapolis.

Spokesmen at all four said they knew nothing about the little boy or the tab collection.

Callahan said she then called Greg Dupree, president of the National Kidney Foundation's Indianapolis chapter.

Dupree told her the whole thing was a hoax and that the foundation had never attempted to establish *collection drives or anything of the sort. Dupree said that the foundation ended a sales drive of Tootsie Rolls candy about 2 weeks ago and that the group would be selling something again in the spring, but that was for the foundation's budget, not for patients.*

In an Associated Press story about the Jackson hoax, a nurse at University of Minnesota's dialysis unit said the rumors seemed to begin about 1969, when dialysis machines and machine operators were scarce in parts of the country. The nurse said people began collecting box tops that could be redeemed for money and sending the money for kidney patients' use.

Callahan said Dupree suggested that the troops continue to collect the tabs and sell them to a recycling center. The proceeds could then be given to the Kidney Foundation for the foundation's use.

The ironic part of the hoax, is that it usually isn't needed. Since 1973, the federal government has covered 80 percent of the costs for dialysis. Most insurance companies will cover the remainder of the costs.

(From the *Muncie Star,* 8 December 1984, p. A-5.)

"The Gay-Jesus Film Petition"

ACTION NEEDED NOW

Modern People News *has revealed plans for the filming of a movie based on the sex life of Jesus, in which Jesus is portrayed as a "swinging homosexual." This film will be shot in the U.S. this year, unless a public outcry is* GREAT. *Already a French prostitute has been named to play the part of Mary Magdalene, with whom Christ has a blatent [sic] affair in the movie. We cannot afford to stand by and do nothing about this disgrace. It is time for us to stand up and be counted! We must not allow this perverted world to drag Our Lord through the dirt. Please Help us to get this film banned from the U.S. as it has been in Europe. Let us show how we feel!*

Detach and mail this form below to the address given. Make copies and give to your friends and others.

(The heading for a form letter and petition circulated in September 1984 by a radio station in Gadsen, Alabama, and sent to me by Bob Sabin of Birmingham.)

The form letter—addressed to the attorney general of Alabama, has this postscript:

Evangelist Jimmy Swaggart recently reported that the above mentioned movie HAS BEEN COMPLETED!!! According to Brother Swaggart, the movie company has released word that the movie is scheduled to be shown in various locations around the country during the Christmas Season. So, the time is short to put a

*stop to it. We sincerely hope that all spiritually and
morally minded people will band together and keep
this UNGODLY type of filth out of Alabama.*

By later the same day the radio station personnel had
attempted to contact *Modern People News* and had been in
touch with the Alabama Attorney General's office. Following these efforts at verification, a statement was read
on the air saying that although the attorney general had
received between two and three thousand letters over a
period of several weeks concerning the supposed gay-
Jesus movie, no evidence could be found that such a
project ever existed. *Modern People News,* it was stated,
seemed to have either gone out of business or changed
their name.

Ann Landers got in on this one in her column of 20
January 1985, which was largely devoted to a long letter
from the attorney general of the State of Illinois, where
Modern Film News, the movie's supposed distributor, had
its headquarters. In Illinois the story circulated as a chain
letter urging people to write to Attorney General Wil-
liam J. Scott's office. But Scott, it turned out, had been
out of office for some four years; thus, the more than one
thousand letters a week on the subject, coming from
forty-one states and a dozen foreign countries, were
being handled by the present administration.

State of Illinois Attorney General Neil F. Hartigan,
harassed by the flood of inquiries, turned to Ann Landers for help in suppressing the story. He had found not
"a shred of truth" to the rumor, and said he had traced
the story to a 1977 issue of a suburban Chicago publication called (surprise!) *Modern People News,* in which the
discussion of such a possible film project in Europe was
mentioned. From that start the idea seems to have grown
into what Ann Landers termed "that wacky chain letter
. . . [with] not an iota of truth in it." The petition sure

sounds like folklore to me. And it *looks* like folklore too, with all those random capital letters, underlines, and exclamation points!!!

Joseph Duffy, an investigator of comparative religions, heresy, and cults, wrote a well-documented analysis of gay-Jesus film rumors for the publication *Media Spotlight* (subtitled "A Biblical Analysis of Entertainment and the Media"—vol. 6, no. 4, October–December 1985). He found that "over one million Christians have written protest letters" but concluded that these "severely misinformed persons" were reacting to nothing but hearsay and error. In the version of the petition that Duffy quotes, the supposed film is actually titled "The Sex Life of Jesus."

According to a story in the *New York Times* (29 September 1985, Arts and Leisure section, p. 1) the rumors that a planned film by director Martin Scorsese, "The Last Temptation of Christ," would portray Jesus as a homosexual contributed to the project being canceled by its backers.

Celebrity Rumors and Legends—A Selection

Celebrities, by definition, are prominent people who are widely "celebrated," or talked about. And a good deal of this talk—which often extends into chatty printed sources—consists of unverified rumors and legends. The folklorist's concern is not with the published gossip-column chit-chat, such as speculations about who's dating whom; or what film, TV, and recording projects are rumored (i.e., leaked by publicists); or what celebrity diets, gurus, or exercises are hot. While it's true that some oral folklore gets into the tabloids and scandal sheets, it's the reports and stories that circulate primarily as anonymous, formularized, traditional *talk* that qualifies for the folklorist's attention.

A number of these folk stories about celebrities were discussed in *The Choking Doberman.* Documented there from the early 1980s were legends about Reggie Jackson on an elevator, Johnny Carson's saucy remarks to his guests, and Burt Reynolds' telephone credit card number. Whatever you heard from a friend of a friend, Reggie did *not* say "sit" to his dog on a New York elevator and scare the daylights out of three midwestern ladies. Nor did Johnny insult Mrs. Arnold Palmer with a crude comment during an on-air interview. Nor did Burt give out his credit card number and invite fans to make free calls. These fetching tales have several variations in personalities or wording, and none can be verified. See my other book for the details.

Here are some examples of further, fairly recent, and very persistent celebrity rumors and legends:

"The Kennedy Note"

Q—*My aunt gave me what she says is an extremely rare commemorative $1 bill, the John F. Kennedy Dallas note. It's a series 1963 Federal Reserve note from the Dallas district and includes a large "K" (apparently for Kennedy) and "11" (apparently for November, the month of his death in 1963). What can you tell me about it?—F.K., Skokie.*

A—*The bill you describe has no relation to the assassination, despite an outlandish rumor that obviously refuses to die. Since the 1930's, an "11" and "K" have designated Federal Reserve notes issued through the Dallas bank, just as "G" and "7" appear on new bills released in the Chicago district. Also, Congress authorized printing of the series 1963 $1 notes in June, 1963, five months before the murder.*

In short, your bill merely is a normal Federal Reserve note that has no special value to collectors.

(An undated clipping, probably from The *Chicago Tribune,* part of a column on "collectibles" under the by-line of Roger Boye.)

JFK lore has been a staple of the rumor mills for years, and it continues to appear steadily, in both printed and oral circulation. The two most common traditions are about a supposed assassination conspiracy or about the notion that President Kennedy is in a coma but being sustained on life-support machines in a secret hideaway. A summary of several other rumors concerning "public personalities who have supposedly survived their announced deaths" is given in Hal Morgan and Kerry Tucker's book *Rumor!* (New York: Penguin, 1984), pp. 103–6, a work in which reference is also made to the "Bozo the Clown" story below. The other side of the surviving-celebrity theme is represented by rumors that a living celebrity has actually died, Paul McCartney of the Beatles being a favorite subject.

"Michael Jackson's Telephone Number"

. . . No one knows why, but the word is sweeping the country that the first seven numbers in the Thriller *album's product code—a 10-digit number above those little bar graphs that appear on the label of just about everything these days—is actually Michael Jackson's phone number.*

It isn't true. Never has been, never will be. The rumor is false. Utterly, completely. Epic Records uses the code number for inventory, nothing else.

Besides, like any multimillionaire worth his Rolls, Mr. J has an unlisted number, in his case in Encino, Calif. Not in Youngstown, Ohio; Franklin, Ohio; Jarrell, Tex.; Contoocook, N.H.; Ocala, Fla; Bradenton, Fla.; Springfield, Ore; Timbo, Ark.; Shafter, Calif., or, to the extreme discomfort of the employees at Bellevue Hair Studio, Bellevue, Wash.

Since mid-December, the hair studio has been flooded with as many as 50 phone calls a day asking if Michael Jackson is there. A few other places in the United States have the same number in their area codes and they too are being besieged. But none are suffering quite like the folks in Bellevue.

. . . A spokesman at Epic Records in Los Angeles said he hadn't heard of the phone number rumor. Some of the callers told the Bellevue hair stylists they'd first heard the rumor on cable television network, MTV. Michael Nadelman, public relations manager for MTV, said the network has never broadcast any such thing.

(From a front-page story by Doug Margeson in the Bellevue, Washington, *Journal-American*, 25 April 1984.)

Nineteen eighty-four was a peak year for Michael Jackson rumors, so much so that spokesmen for the singer called a press conference in Hollywood on 5 September specifically to deny several of them. No, they said, Michael is not gay, he had never taken hormones to maintain his high voice, nor had his cheekbones or eyes ever been surgically modified in any way (though his nose had been narrowed some years before). The news reports of the press conference did not mention whether the other popular rumors were denied that Jackson supposedly sang the high notes on some of Diana Ross's recordings, that his telephone number is printed on the *Thriller* album (see above), or that his dancing partner in the Pepsi commercial had died (see below). OK—that's enough! Leave the guy alone!

"Michael Jackson's Dancing Partner"

*—Is there any truth to the rumor we keep hearing
about the young dancer in the Michael Jackson
commercial breaking his neck while break dancing?
My nieces are so upset.*

*—By now they should have seen news stories
refuting the tall tale that Alfonso Ribeiro, 12, had
died. Where the rumor started is unknown, but it was
suddenly in schools all over the country, spread by
kids who insisted they had heard it on TV. (In some
places, the rumor was he died of a drug overdose; in
others he had been hit by a motorcycle while riding
his bike; the break-dancing story was the one told
most often.)*

*If it's any comfort to Ribeiro, the stories are a sure
sign he's made it. Why kids like to spread such false,
ghoulish stories, is hard to figure, but it's happened
to every young performer popular with adolescents
since Annette Funicello during her* Mickey Mouse
Club *days.*

(From Bettelou Peterson's "The Viewers Ask" column, distributed by Knight-Ridder newspapers, as published in the *Houston Post,* TV Week section, 22 July
1984.)

"Bozo the Clown's Blooper"

Version A: *The "Bozo the Clown" show aired in Los Angeles in the late 1950s and early 60s. On one show a group of children are playing a game in which they are supposed to carry an egg in a spoon across the room. One small boy drops his egg halfway across, whereupon he utters a graphic expression of disgust. When Bozo the Clown gently reprimands the youngster, he is told by the disgruntled tyke to "shove it," or worse. I have at least a half-dozen friends who claim to have witnessed the show but are always vague as to even its approximate date and the exact language used.*

(In a letter from John R. Witkowski of Los Angeles, dated 11 November 1984.)

Version B: *This supposedly occurred on the Baltimore version of the "Bozo the Clown" show about twenty years ago when it was done live. Bozo was interviewing the kids—asking them how old they are, what they'd like to be when they grow up, all the typical stuff—when he gets to this one boy who answers him with "Ram it, clown!" Naturally, the show is cut off for a few minutes with "technical difficulties." When it returns, the boy is gone and order has been restored.*

I accepted this as gospel until I moved to New Orleans. After a particularly ugly session with our boss, my co-worker said (after the boss was out of earshot), "Ram it, clown!" I was stunned. I asked him where he got that from, and he told me the same story except, of course, that it was the New Orleans version of the "Bozo" show.

(In a letter from Douglas J. Kaplan of New Orleans, dated 13 December 1984.)

A similar blooper story: *A children's-television-show host was taken off the air after he said, "That ought to shut the little bastards up!" on live television during what he thought was a commercial break. (1960s)*
Not true. The statement was attributed, in different versions of the tale, to virtually every local children's-show host around the country. Despite a complete lack of supporting evidence—no one telling the story had ever seen the episode themselves—the myth was widely believed. Many who heard it as children still consider the story a fact.

(From Morgan and Tucker's *Rumor!,* p. 92.)

To tell the truth, I always thought that the host of my own favorite kids' *radio* show, "Happy Hank" (heard in Lansing, Michigan, mid-1940s), had spoken these naughty words into a live mike. And I was pretty sure too that some urchin had sassed back Lansing radio host "Uncle Howdy," another childhood favorite, right on the air. After all, would my best buddies of grade school lie? *They* all believed it too. But age and experience and dozens of accounts like the three quoted above convinced me that these are traditional versions of broadcasting history as people think it *should be,* not as it really was.

"The Dolly Parton Diet"—A Journalistic Odyssey

Times were slow. We were starved for a good story. Then came a hot flash from Detroit—a new diet was all the rage in the Midwest, reducing dozens of women to better proportions.

Instead of being named after an "in" place . . . this latest secret to slimness was named after an "in" performer, Dolly Parton.

Our informer was my editor's sister, Ceci, who lives in suburban Detroit. Ceci had tried the diet for two weeks, successfully shed several pounds, and was amazed that we sophisticated New Yorkers hadn't heard of it yet.

"Find out how it started," my editor instructed me.

So I called Dolly. Perhaps she had devised the diet or it had been created for her. She would tell me, I would report back to the editor, and we would explain it in a few words.

But few assignments are ever so simple—and this one turned out to be even more puzzling than most.

Dolly was incommunicado, off writing music. . . . I settled for her publicists and manager's assistant. All insisted that there is no such thing as a "Dolly Parton Diet."

"Whoever started it is using the name illegally," said Dolly's assistant manager. "Dolly has neither heard of it nor does she endorse it."

. . . I returned to the only source who was willing to tell all, my editor's sister Ceci.

Ceci was at work, couldn't remember the diet verbatim, and asked me to call her at home later. "It's

right on top of the refrigerator. If I'm not home,
someone can read it to you."

I phoned that night. Ceci was out, so, as directed, I
asked her husband if he would dictate the diet from
the refrigerator. "There's something there called 'The
Stewardess Diet,' " he reported. "Is that it?"

I called again later. Ceci giggled and—finally—read
me what was labeled the "Dolly Parton Diet." I
pressed her to remember its origin.

Ceci thought hard. She had run across the diet
several times, she said. The first time was a
conversation overheard in the sauna of the Lady
Health Spa. . . .

She heard mention of it a few times after that and
once even spotted it posted in a kitchen she happened
to visit while helping her daughter look for an
off-campus apartment in East Lansing, Mich. Finally
she secured a copy from a friend, Mary Schweitzer,
when the two families were at a baseball game
together. Ceci promised to get me Mary's phone
number.

To save time, I called all the Schweitzers in the
Detroit phone book, and eventually got a Mary. But
she was the wrong one. . . .

Realizing that I had arrived at a temporary dead
end, I switched my approach, and called the only
person I know in Detroit—my cousin Andy, who
usually is up on all the latest trends.

Sure enough, Andy had struggled through the diet
about two months ago, "mainly because I thought it
would enlarge my bust," she joked. "Of course, it
didn't."

She had heard of the Dolly diet from a country-club
pal, Shirleen King. . . .

Pal Shirleen had . . . gone on the diet for two

weeks and lost seven pounds. Her husband had even photocopied and distributed copies to numerous friends and associates.

Shirleen had learned about it from another couple who were members of the same country club. Their names were Blanche and Norbert Ketai.

I called Blanche next. She had discovered the diet at her beauty parlor. "My husband and I were on it for seven days," she reported. "He lost seven pounds. I lost five. . . . I gave it to at least 10 people, all my friends. Everyone I know is talking about it. I always collect diets and pass them along."

But she couldn't remember the name of her beauty parlor source. She suggested I phone another country-club friend, Ceil Singer, who may have picked up a copy from a different source. I did. Singer, too, reported that a bunch of friends had been on the diet. But Singer had no further source for me to tap.

Another dead end. This sleuthing was tougher than I expected. By now, my only hope was my editor's sister's friend, Mary Schweitzer.

Ceci came through for us. She dug around and learned that her friend Mary had heard of it from her adopted daughter, Maureen Scott, who in turn got it from a friend in Akron, Robin Perron. Ceci even had Robin's home and work numbers. . . .

Eagerly, I began making Akron connections, starting with Robin. . . . She had distributed the Parton diet to various friends and roommates, after receiving her copy from another roommate Ginny Miller.

The three roommates, who were all at Akron University, found it somewhat difficult to diet and still maintain their hectic schedules, but each stayed with it for a week, and each lost six pounds or so.

My next step was to talk to Ginny. She explained

that she had heard of the diet from still another roommate, Sue Van Buren, who had worked for the Board of Elections in Akron last year, when, she said, the Dolly diet was going around in a big way.

Tracking right along, I dialed the Board of Elections and spoke with one of Sue's former co-workers, who explained that another former associate, Frank Cieriello, had brought the diet to his colleagues. Cieriello had since been transferred to the city auditor's office.

I pressed on and located Frank. He thought for a few minutes and recalled that Gladys Lucas, who also had worked at the board, had told him about the diet seven months ago.

Getting hold of Gladys was tricky because she was out every time I phoned. Finally I asked her husband, Dwight, about the diet. He thought their daughter had come across it when working at Akron General Hospital, but because he wasn't sure, he asked me to check back. So I did. Hourly. At last, Gladys came home, and explained that she had given copies of the diet to at least 15 people, if not more. But her source was her daughter Joan.

I called Joan Lucas.

"How weird," Joan said when I explained my call. She had been in Detroit visiting her boyfriend, Jim Hussey, over the New Year weekend, she recalled. "At one party, I met this guy who told me how he had been on this diet for six weeks and lost 50 pounds. It sounded good to me, so I wrote it down. I can't remember his name."

I asked if her boyfriend would, and she said he might. "Call and ask him for Leo's dad's phone number," she advised.

So after all that I was back in Detroit. When I called Jim to obtain Leo's dad's number, Jim informed me that everyone he knew had been on the diet the past year, that it was old news and that he himself had received copies from three or four different friends. He didn't have Leo's dad's number, but he gave me his name, Joe Norbito.

Unfortunately, Leo is away. Joe is not listed with Detroit information. So I am dead-ended again. Unless someone knows Joe and can tell me how to reach him.

I convinced my editor that after interrogating close to 50 persons about this, enough is enough. After all, we have the diet. . . .

(By Ricki Fulman of the *New York News,* as reprinted in the *Chicago Tribune,* Lifestyle section, p. 1, on 13 September 1981, and sent to me by Robert Shuster of Wheaton, Illinois.)

I don't usually do diets. But this is such a fine example of the pervasiveness of a celebrity legend and the dogged determination of a reporter to track it down that I have quoted most of the story. The diet itself consists basically of one food per day, all you want, along with unlimited portions of "T. J.'s Miracle Soup." But, according to Fulman, "No one knows who T. J. is, in case you're wondering."

Legends of Academe

An excellent survey of the folk traditions of academe by Professor (and folklorist) Barre Toelken appears in Appendix B of my textbook *The Study of American Folklore* (New York: W. W. Norton, 2nd. ed., 1978). Toelken touches on such varied forms as campus slang, superstitions surrounding exams and athletics, anecdotes about the faculty, a ritual for announcing an engagement, and several urban legends typically known by college and university students. Most of the legends—like "The Spider in the Hairdo" and "The Death Car"—are transplants from high-school lore; but others—such as the stories about fatal fraternity initiations, medical students' grotesque pranks, or the desperate survival tactics devised by law students—are indigenous to the campus and reflect esoteric subcultures within the general framework of campus life.

The entire subject of campus folklore deserves a book of its own, so I give here only representative examples of three well-known legend themes: the eccentric faculty member, the artful examination cheater, and the nature of life (and death) in the college dormitory.

"The Acrobatic Professor"

Dr. Frederic Coenen at the University of North Carolina told the story of Meno Spann, a former professor at Chapel Hill, who told his classes that he never gave pop quizzes except on the days when he came in the classroom through the transom. Naturally, the students were pleased until he carried out his threat—usually once a semester—and came in through the transom.

(Quoted by Oliver Finley Graves in "Folklore in Academe: The Anecdote of the Professor and the Transom," *Indiana Folklore* 12 [1979], pp. 142–45; as he heard it told that same year by two foreign-language instructors at the University of Alabama. The following two variants are also from Graves's article.)

Dr. Guy Y. Williams reigned for almost 40 years as the [University of Oklahoma] chemistry department's most colorful professor. A former circus performer, he enjoyed surprising students with his acrobatic skills.

The most famous Guy Y. story, which still circulates in the corridors of DeBarr Hall, had to do with transoms and pop quizzes. It is claimed that he told a long-ago class of chemistry students he never gave pop quizzes. He promised that the day he gave a pop quiz would be the day he came to class through the transom. The tale, of course, has Williams entering his classroom one day via the transom route before administering a pop quiz to his startled students.

Williams himself denied the pop quiz story, according to Dr. Bernard Heston, former chair of the chemistry department. *But Williams did admit to Heston that he entered classrooms on more than one occasion through the transom.*

(Quoted by Graves from the October 1979 issue of *The Sooner,* published by the Oklahoma Alumni Association, in an article titled "Unorthodox Profs Enliven OU History.")

Asked the oft-repeated query at the end of his lecture—whether he planned to give a quiz the next day—a professor at Mississippi State University answered nonchalantly, "A quiz? Why, I'd climb through that transom over the door before I'd give a quiz tomorrow." A sigh of relief passed through the classroom. But next day, after the class had assembled, there was a sudden clamor outside the door. The transom began to creak open and, to the utter amazement of the students, in climbed their professor—grinning happily and clutching a three-page quiz in his hand.

(Quoted by Graves from the "Campus Comedy" section in the October 1961 issue of *Reader's Digest.*)

Dr. Ralph Doty of the University of Oklahoma Classics Department looked further into the Guy Y. Williams version, which has the most supporting detail associated with it. He heard a variation on the story going around campus in 1983: students supposedly had locked Professor Williams out of his classroom once when he was late, but he came in over the transom (as threatened) and then gave them a pop quiz (as promised).

Checking Williams's obituary in the *Oklahoma Daily* (1 February 1968), Doty learned that although the professor was said to have been a circus acrobat at the age of twenty-nine, and occasionally to have entertained classes by performing a one-handed handstand on his desk, no reference whatever to coming in over the transom was made here or in an earlier *Oklahoman* interview with Professor Williams. Consulting a biographical sketch in a history of the University of Oklahoma published in 1942, Doty learned that Guy Williams had moved quite steadily through his undergraduate and graduate education and had gone directly into teaching after graduation. In his twenty-ninth year, according to the book, he was on sabbatical leave in Chicago.

However, former students' testimonies contradict the published reports. Dr. Doty interviewed Dorothy Dufran, who, along with her husband, J. B. Dufran, had been in Guy Y. Williams's Chemistry 101 class during the period 1946–48. Mrs. Dufran remembered Dr. Williams making his pop quiz/transom promise at the beginning of the course *and* of his actually entering through the transom twice during the semester she was in the class. On both occasions, she recalled, the door was closed but not locked, and no attempt was made by students to bar him from the classroom. Furthermore, Mrs. Dufran reports, as Dr. Doty writes, "her mother, now deceased, took Chemistry 101 from Dr. Williams in 1925 and was given a pop quiz when the professor climbed through the transom." Either we have—at last—hit upon the actual origin of a legend of academe, or else there have been three (at least) acrobatic professors performing identical stunts for identical reasons.*

---

*Make that *five.* Hal Heisler of Los Angeles wrote me on 3 September 1985 that when he was a freshman at Union College in Schenectady, New York, Orin James Farrell, Professor of Mathematics, entered the classroom one day over the transom and commenced handing out surprise-quiz papers, as earlier promised. Then Charles D. Aulds wrote me on 27 September 1985 that about 1980 or 1981, at Tennessee Technological University in Cookeville, a history professor, "Jumpin' " J. B. Clark, said to be an accomplished acrobat,

At the University of Utah the story is told about a music professor entering class one day by climbing out of a grand piano where he had hidden before the students arrived. When a folklore student of mine asked the man about this story, he said only, "Have you ever looked to see how much space there is between the cover and the strings of a grand piano?" Well—there's not much room there—I know. But this guy is quite small, and I heard that he had been a contortionist in a carnival as a young man.

---

entered a classroom through a ground-floor window and started distributing pop quiz papers. Incidentally, Jim Mehl of Los Gatos, California, wrote me on 4 September 1985 that when he was an undergraduate at the University of Oklahoma from 1957 to 62, students still remembered the transom story about "Guy Wire Williams."

Blue Book Legends (Versions A through F)

A. *This student went into his final examination with an A- average. There were two essay questions. He knew nothing about the first one, but he was primed on the second. He filled his first blue book with just anything he thought of. Then he labeled his second blue book II and began it with what appeared to be the last sentence or two of the answer to the first essay question. Then on the second page of this second blue book he put down 2 for the second essay question, and he wrote a beautiful answer. He turned in only the second blue book. A few days later he got a postcard from the instructor saying he got an A in the course and apologizing for having lost the first blue book.*

(Quoted by Lew Girdler in "The Legend of the Second Blue Book," *Western Folklore* 29 [1970], pp. 111–13; as he heard it in 1937 from a Berkeley graduate student. The next two variations are also from Girdler's article.)

B. *The student takes a test which is composed of two pages. Realizing that he doesn't know much, he spends all his time on the second page. When the period ends, he slips the first page into his notebook and only hands in the second page.*

Once outside the classroom, he hurriedly looks up the answers and fills in the first page. Then he takes and steps on the page. He gives this page to a friend who [has] a later class in the same room. The friend approaches the teacher after class and says that he found this "in the back." The teacher takes it, checks through the papers collected in the morning class,

and sure enough, the student's first page is missing.
He grades all the papers and the student gets an A.

(Quoted by Girdler as written out for him by a student
at San Jose State College who had heard it told in 1960
as something that had happened the year before.)

C. *A friend of mine tells this about her brother*
Jack, a sometime student. Jack found himself sitting in
the classroom during an important examination with
two blue books, a pen, and a question he couldn't
answer. Being naturally bright, if lazy, he thought of
the following solution. In one of the blue books he
wrote a letter to his mother, telling her that he had
finished writing his exam early but was waiting for a
friend in the same class and so was taking the
opportunity to write to her. He apologized for not
writing sooner but said he'd been studying very hard
for this instructor, who was a nice guy but had pretty
high standards. When the time was up he handed in
this blue book and left in a hurry with his unused
one. He hurried to his text, wrote an answer, and
then put the blue book in an envelope and mailed it
to his mother in Boston. When the instructor found
the letter he called Jack, who explained that he had
written in two blue books and must have got them
mixed up, and if the instructor had the letter, the
answer must be in the mail on the way to Boston. He
offered to call his mother in Boston and have her
send the envelope back as soon as she got it. He did,
she did, and the blue book was sent back, with the
inner envelope postmarked the day of the test and the
outer envelope postmarked Boston.

(Quoted by Girdler as written out for him by a student
at San Jose State College in 1967.)

D. *I really did read this story in the paper—*
sometime in 1976 or 1977, either in the Daily Bruin
(UCLA's paper) or the L. A. Times.

A chemistry professor at UCLA is conducting a final
exam. He is an extremely difficult professor, and a bit
of an S.O.B. He has told his students that all writing
must *stop when he calls time—anyone who doesn't*
stop will automatically fail the exam. The class is in a
large auditorium and is required for all chemistry,
biology, etc. students. At the end all the students
except one finish as instructed. The one student keeps
writing furiously for 30 seconds or so until he is
stopped by the professor, who tells him he has failed
the exam.

The student walks to the front of the room with his
blue book and attempts to argue. The professor
doesn't budge, so finally the student takes a very
arrogant attitude and says, "Do you know who I am?"
The professor sneers and says, "No, I don't, and it
wouldn't matter," whereupon the student says
"Great!" sticks his blue book into the middle of the
stack of blue books already turned in, and runs out of
the room.

(As written out and sent to me by Cindy Burnham of
Memphis, Tennessee, August 1984. See the next example for another version.)

D-. *I heard one at Cornell in late 1980 that sounds*
too good to be true. . . . A graduate student claimed
it occurred during his undergraduate days in Ithaca.
At the close of a final exam, the proctor announced
time was up and directed the students to turn their
blue books in. One student, hastening to finish a
thought, kept scribbling. Finishing, he rushed to the
front of the room and handed in his exam book, one
of the last to do so. The proctor said, "I won't accept

this," and the flabbergasted student asked why. "I told everyone to stop and you kept on going. I can't accept it." The student was aghast. "What'll happen then?" "You'll probably flunk," shrugged the proctor. With that, the student drew himself up proudly and asked, "Do you know who I am?" Unimpressed, the proctor answered, "No." The student replied, "Good," and jammed his blue book into the center of the pile on the desk.

(As written out and sent to me by Howard Baldwin of Palo Alto, California, June 1984.)

F. *This story was current when I was an undergraduate and I must confess to being completely taken in by it until I heard it from friends who had attended different universities. The informant is usually "someone who was a student here a few years ago." It seems that a final year student was worried that he would be unable to do enough revision [i.e., review] for his forthcoming exams, so began taking "speed" to enable him to go without sleep and work through the night. He did this for about two or three weeks before the exams. The fateful day arrived. Our hero took a shot and entered the examination room. Once at his desk he got through the paper in record time and left feeling confident that he had answered every question brilliantly.*

A few days later he was called in to see his personal tutor. "How did you feel the exam went?" he was asked. "Like a dream," he replied. "Well in that case," said his tutor, "perhaps you'd care to explain why you covered thirty sheets of paper with your own name?"

(As written out and sent to me by David Kennedy of Leicester, England, January 1985. In his article "The

Folklore of Colleges" in *The American Mercury* [vol. 68, 1949] Richard Dorson mentioned a story about a "coed" at the University of Minnesota taking a final examination after drinking several cocktails. She went to the wrong classroom but managed to earn a grade of B for the political science course she had never attended and got an incomplete grade for the one in American literature for which she failed to appear for the final. A parallel tradition is the story of a driver stopped by the state police on a freeway. He has been taking some kind of drug, and was observed "speeding" down the highway— really going about five miles per hour.)

Dorm Life (and Death)
"The Surprise"

Two roommates had taken to pulling crude pranks on each other in the dorm. It happened that one lazy Sunday afternoon one of the roommates had gone down the hall from his room to take a shower. His fellow roommate was in the room studying when there was a knock on the door and the showering roommate's father, who had driven down for a visit, came in bringing with him the girlfriend of the showerer and his mother. The folks were quite naturally invited into the room and they commenced to chat. The other roommate was quite taken with the girlfriend, and he did not go and get his friend, likely assuming he would return soon—which he did. He was clad only in a towel, which he threw off as opened the door and barged in; with his hand gripping his penis, he screamed, "Bang, bang; you're dead!"

(As written out and sent to me in September 1984 by Robert W. Haskett of Flagstaff, Arizona, as remembered from Indiana University in the early 1960s.)

A second version of this well-known campus story was sent to me in November 1983 by David Shannon, who remembered it from Cornell University in 1966. Mr. Shannon wrote to me at the time from his position with the Foster Parents Plan in Kathmandu, Nepal. How that campus folklore does get around!

♣"The Roommate's Death"

*There were once two girls who were supposed to
be staying in a dormitory over Christmas vacation,
and everyone else had already left, and the dorm
director had left, and they were the only two girls
who would be staying there. Well, the dorm director
before she left told them, told the two girls, to make
sure that they keep all the doors locked and don't
answer the door for anyone during the evening
because there was supposed to be a hatchet man . . .
he was supposed to be out. So the girls promised, of
course, you know, because they didn't want to get
hurt either.*

*So it was late one night, and one girl was upstairs
. . . it wasn't a very big dorm . . . they had kind of a
library-study downstairs, and one girl was upstairs in
her room, and the other one wanted to go down to
study, and the one girl said, "Well, I really don't
think you should, but, well, if you want to go down
there, well, go ahead, but be very, very careful, and
be sure the door is locked."*

*So the girl went downstairs, and it got rather late.
It was about 12:00 or 12:30, and the girl upstairs
heard this very funny, heavy noise like someone
walking, kind of dragging themselves up the steps.
And, of course, she was a little bit shook. She didn't
know what was going on, so she grabbed her desk
and some other things and shoved them against the
door, and this draggin', heavy draggin' feet just
started walking, and she could hear it coming down
the hall toward her room. Of course she was
panic-stricken; she didn't know what to do, so she just*

kept pushing things against the door and standing by it and had it locked and everything so that nobody could get in.

Well, the dragging steps just came closer and closer and stopped by the door, and whoever it was started scratching at the door . . . started gnawing at it and kept scratching and wouldn't stop. Well, she was absolutely horror-stricken, and she went in the corner and just sat there and just kinda cringed up in the corner. The scratching continued for a long time, and then suddenly it just stopped. And, well, she didn't want to open the door or anything, so she just left it that way, and she stayed that way the whole night. She was kinda cuddled up in the corner by her bed . . . in the corner of the room.

Then the next morning when she woke up she didn't hear anything, so she figured it's daylight, and she couldn't figure out what happened to her roommate. She didn't know what had happened to her, and she figured, well, something must have happened. So she thought she better go down and find out, so she took all the things away from the door.

When she opened the door, she saw her roommate with a hatchet in her head. She was the one that was scratching at the door, trying to get in so she could be saved. And if she would have made it in time, she probably could have saved her or done something.

(This is text number 278 in Ronald L. Baker's *Hoosier Folk Legends* [Bloomington: Indiana University Press, 1982], pp. 217–18; as told in 1968 by a student from Hammond, Indiana.)

This campus favorite has been well documented by folklorists back to 1961, and it is probably even older. It combines the sound effects and horror of ♣"The Boy-friend's Death" and a specific campus setting. Some versions also incorporate an element from the legend I call ✈"The Licked Hand," in which the murderer's mocking message is written in blood on the bathroom mirror or wall. In "The Licked Hand" the young woman feels her hand being licked during the night by, presumably, her trusty pet dog. But the bloody note she reads by the dawn's early light says "People Can Lick Too."

AFTERWORD

Why Should It Ever End?

Urban legends seem to go on and on, whether new ones, old ones, or the renewed forms of old legends. In order to fill their niche in modern tradition, stories need not be true but merely believable; and they need not even be *that* plausible, just as long as they are ironic, suspenseful, or funny. Rule 1: The truth never stands in the way of a good story.

I fully expect that people will continue to listen to urban legends, repeat them, vary them, and somehow mysteriously invent them in the future, just as they have for so many years in the past. Even our government may get involved in the legend-making process, as the following recent news story suggests:

U.S. MAY CONCOCT TALES OF HORROR
TO DETER TRESPASS AT NUCLEAR SITE

CANYONLANDS NATIONAL PARK, *Utah—The federal government is considering getting into the business of making up horror stories.*

Here's the problem: There's a good chance that a square mile of desert adjacent to this park will become a dump for high-level nuclear wastes that will remain dangerous for 10,000 years.

Signs probably won't last that long, so the Office of Nuclear Waste Isolation, a branch of the Department of Energy, is looking for ways to deter future trespassers.

A consultant to the agency, Thomas A. Sebeok, a linguistics and anthropology professor at the University of Indiana,* came up with a novel idea: Invent "curse of the Pharoah" type myths that will literally keep people scared away. He included his advice in a 33-page technical report titled "Communications Measures to Bridge 10 Millennia."

The myths would be "tantamount to laying a false trail, meaning the uninitiated will be steered away from the hazardous site for reasons other than scientific knowledge."

The myths, according to Mr. Sebeok, would be laid down and kept alive by a special "atomic priesthood" created by the Energy Department and comprised of scientists and scholars. The priesthood would be "self-perpetuating," he adds.

"When one member dies, the others would choose to initiate a replacement," Mr. Sebeok says.

The 64-year-old professor says he came up with the idea by watching old "monster movies" about archeologists who meet tragedy when they violate the sacred tombs of Egyptian Pharaohs. He concedes that such curses, in reality, haven't always worked; the looting of many Egyptian tombs is proof.

So he suggests that nuclear-dump myths should be used only as a supplementary method to the more normal methods to keep trespassers away, such as fences and gates.

---

*It's really "Indiana University"; I know, because I studied folklore there.

How the myths would be spread is another problem, Mr. Sebeok says, although he adds that there are the conventional "folkloristic devices," such as word of mouth.

Indeed, if Mr. Sebeok succeeds, maybe art will follow life following art. How about "Indiana Jones and the Department of Energy"?

(A story under the byline Con Psarras in the *Wall Street Journal,* 25 June 1984.)

INDEX